Art and the Stage

A THEMES IN ART BOOK

Published by The Cleveland Museum of Art
in cooperation with Indiana University Press

Art and the Stage

ELLEN BREITMAN

Cover

23 William Nicholson, *Sarah Bernhardt*.

Title Page

35 Jean Béraud, *Valmy and Lea* (detail).

Copyright 1981 by The Cleveland Museum of Art
11150 East Boulevard, Cleveland, Ohio 44106

Distributed by Indiana University Press
Bloomington, Indiana 47401

Library of Congress Cataloging in Publication Data
Breitman, Ellen, 1951-
  Art and the stage.
  Catalog of an exhibition held at the Cleveland
Museum of Art, May 22-Aug. 16, 1981.
    Theaters—Stage–setting and scenery—Exhibitions.
2. Ballet—Stage–setting and scenery—Exhibitions.
3. Costume—Exhibitions. 4. Playbills—Exhibitions.
5. Actors—Portraits—Exhibitions. I. Cleveland
Museum of Art. II. Title.
PN 2086.B7   792'.025'074017132   81–4090
ISBN 0–910386–64–1 (pbk.)   AACR2

Contents

Lenders to the Exhibition

Allen Memorial Art Museum
Anonymous
Mrs. Noah L. Butkin
The Butler Institute of American Art
The Cleveland Museum of Art
Columbus Museum of Art
Joseph M. Erdelac
Special Collections Department,
    Northwestern University Library
Theatre Arts Area,
    Cleveland State University
The Western Reserve Historical Society

Acknowledgements

In surprisingly many ways, mounting a museum exhibition—complete with the preparation of a book-catalog—is not unlike producing a stage performance. As one would expect from any creative endeavor, a considerable amount of planning and coordination is required. Beyond this, however, exhibitions and stage productions share similar characteristics: both have limited runs, often with special opening-night previews; both play to an audience on which they depend for appreciation, support, and ultimate realization; both require a cast of characters; and for both, the element of design plays a crucial role in the clear, meaningful, and decorative presentation of ideas and images. Even after closing, whether exhibition or stage production, the show lives on: in the catalog or script, the reviews, the photographs, and the indelible memories.

Perhaps the one factor which most accounts for the success of an exhibition or stage production is its cast of characters. In *Art and the Stage*, as in any exhibition, the objects themselves make up the "onstage" cast. But it is the "offstage" players who deserve recognition here. To all of them I offer my sincere appreciation and gratitude.

Undoubtedly, the show could never have gone on without the impetus provided by Gabriel P. Weisberg, Curator of Art History and Education, and the backing of Sherman E. Lee, Director of The Cleveland Museum of Art. Throughout the production—more than a year in the making—Dr. Weisberg's well-timed humor served to reinforce the invaluable advice and support he offered.

The Art History and Education Department staff contributed significantly to the overall effort. Janet Leonard, Assistant, was helpful in countless ways— particularly in pinpointing various procedures. Marlene Goldheimer deserves special mention for her patient, cheerful—even enthusiastic—typing of the manuscript from its earliest, most illegible draft to the final version. Martin Linsey (now retired) and his successor, Sheila Webb, share photographic credits with Nicholas Hlobeczy, Museum Photographer, and David Heald, Assistant Photographer. Acknowledgement should also go to Bernice Spink and to my fellow instructors for making adjustments in the teaching schedule when the demands of writing kept me at my desk.

Besides lending posters and making available time, transportation, and space, Andrew Chakalis and his able staff in the Extensions Division of the Department of Art History and Education offered insight and inspiration throughout the development of the show. The Library staff headed by Jack Perry Brown—particularly Judith Frost, Bonnie Postlethwaite, and Sara Jane Pearman— not only funneled books, clippings, and slides in my direction but also smilingly tackled any question I could come up with.

Of course, there would be no show without the generous contributions of the lenders, who are listed elsewhere. Loans from the museum's Departments of Prints and Drawings, and Modern Art were substantial.

Louise Richards, Curator of Prints and Drawings, and staff members in that department—Anne Lockhart, Kim Stapleton Clift, and Karen Smith—were extremely helpful in every way. Certain individuals went beyond providing objects for the show: Russell Maylone, Curator of the Special Collections Department, Northwestern University Library in Evanston, made available the library's full resources and staff; and Reuben Silver, Head of the Theatre Arts Area at Cleveland State University in Cleveland, was willing to share not only a set of study models but also his knowledge of and enthusiasm for theater.

The exhibition in its earliest form as a list of objects and a series of photographs received the careful, perceptive consideration of the Registrar, Delbert Gutridge, and his staff, and the Assistant Designer, Joseph Finizia. The study models received special attention from the Conservation Department, particularly Bruce Christman, and from electrician Peter Rivera. The Textiles Department provided assistance with the costume pieces. An expert crew installed and dismantled the show.

This book remains. From within and around its lines and images so beautifully designed by Chief Editor Merald E. Wrolstad echo the editorial comments of Associate Editors Jo Zuppan, who initially read the manuscript, and Sally W. Goodfellow, who edited the manuscript. Mrs. Goodfellow not only looked for the essence of my ideas and skillfully polished the language used to express them but also patiently attended to numerous, sometimes-harried details—always maintaining a calm, positive demeanor.

To all of these people behind the scenes and to those persons who contributed to the making of this exhibition and catalog by mere virtue of their willingness to listen and offer words of encouragement, I dedicate this book.

Ellen Breitman
March 1981

Introduction

The lure of the stage has continually captured the attention of visual artists. Throughout the history of the theater artists have been instrumental in recording outstanding sets and players from the ephemeral world of the stage production. Sharing our role as spectators, artists have succumbed to the glamour of talented performers as well as to the fascinating range of imagery within the walls of most theaters—from dramatic lighting and colorful sets and costumes to the facial expressions of performers and spectators. Beyond this, a basic conviction that theater, like art, illuminates the human experience has inspired artists not only to observe but also to participate in the theatrical realm. Painters and sculptors have contributed directly to the visual life of stage performances by designing the sets, costumes, programs, and announcements. Paintings, drawings, prints and study models reveal some of the ways artists, as observers or participants, have approached the world of the stage.

The relationships between the performing arts and the visual arts are varied and numerous; it is not our intention to enumerate them all. Artists' interpretations of texts, or their roles as performers in more recent times,[1] form the basis of entirely different studies. The fundamental element of concern here is the stage itself. As a miniature world conveying aspects of real-life drama and comedy, the stage offers for scrutiny meaningful characters or experiences in the same manner as a realistic painting. Or, using a playwright's poetic license,

an artist's creative vision, the unique personal style of an actor, and the interpretive sensibilities of a director, the stage becomes a small arena for bringing to life an inner world of emotion, imagination, and thought. For purposes of continuity, the organizing principle of this book reflects the development of a stage production as seen by various artists from its inception to its ultimate realization in the actual performance.

Stage designs represent one of the visual by-products of theater. Like the architect's plans, however, they serve as the basis and initial phase in the creation of something concrete. They are not intended as permanent works of art. This characteristic of stage designs, plus the transient nature of the production for which they are created, offers an opportunity for experimentation, in freeing the artist to explore ideas about the dynamic and expressive qualities of color, form, or space. Picasso, whose work for the theater is thoroughly studied in Douglas Cooper's *Picasso Theatre* (New York: Harry N. Abrams, 1967), tested in three dimensions his Analytical Cubism and an interest in collage with his designs for costumes and settings in Serge Diaghilev's Ballets Russes' production of Erik Satie's *Parade* (1917).[2] While Picasso's involvement in this and other stage productions was all-encompassing and reflected his personal fascination in the world of performance, when asked to contribute his designs to an exhibition of theater art, he responded that he couldn't be bothered to look for them—indicating the relatively unimportant role he felt they played in his work.[3] Still, the stage designs of artists can enrich not only the stage production itself and the artist's oeuvre but also the art world in which the artist works. Such was the case, for example, when the vibrant designs of Natalie Gontcharova contributed to the revitalization of native Russian art and theater, around the turn of the twentieth century.

Once the stage designs are developed and the opening date has been set, with a unifying concept of what a particular performance will encompass, the stage designer (or a selected artist) summons his creative talents to announce the production to the public. Toward this end, enlightened producers such as Sarah Bernhardt, who contracted with Alphonse Mucha to design posters for her Théâtre de la Renaissance, recognized the effective advertising accomplished with a poster's stylization of a play's content and its female star.

If the images of celebrities called the public into the theaters, music halls, and cabarets, then watching those celebrities—or even anonymous players onstage—was, and remains, an important part of the theatrical experience for the spectator and the artist. Just such an experience had drawn Degas into the rehearsal halls and backstage where he could study a ballerina's form and movement, and had exposed Toulouse-Lautrec to the world of popular Parisian entertainment from which he extracted memorable faces and personalities.

Finally, with the performance about to begin or already in progress, the artist, seated in the audience, observed and skillfully recorded the overall scene. Perhaps he might focus on the visual effects of artificial and dramatic lighting, abstracting form and image—as Seurat did in his concert drawings; or he might choose to depict players on the stage or certain characters in the audience, in either case alluding to the connections between the artificial world of performance and the real life of its spectators. Additionally, the audience experience might inspire the artist to use dramatic lighting or characterization in non-theatrical subjects. Or, coming full circle, it might encourage the artist to seek active participation in stage production—as in the case of Everett Shinn.

The designs, announcements, and representations of the players and audience presented here cover the modern period—particularly around the turn of the twentieth century—when parallel developments in both the visual arts and performing arts were characterized by frenzied activity and innovation. The ramifications of collaborative efforts at that time among the leading producers, directors, writers, performers, composers, and artists were carried further later in the century and indeed are still being explored today.[4]

Focused as it is on the turn of the century, this study makes no claims of being a comprehensive survey. Rather it examines the fundamental nature of stage production through the artist's eyes and involvement, shedding light on the broad range of possibilities by interpreting selected examples. Just as the single production may encourage repeated visits to the theater, this study serves as the point of departure for a continued examination of this interdisciplinary theme.

1. Contemporary performance art—with its roots in the riotous soirées and happenings of the Futurists, Dadaists, and Surrealists early in the century—grew out of the equally irreverent happenings of the 1960s staged by leading American artists such as Robert Rauschenberg, Claes Oldenburg, and Allan Kaprow. Produced in galleries, in the streets, or almost anywhere except on stage in traditional theaters, artists' performances comprise a special category of theater.

While not immediately relevant to this study, happenings, staged events, and recent performance art represent perhaps the ultimate union of the visual and performing arts. Documentation and critical literature is extensive; the reader is referred to the notes and suggestions for further reading in Adrian Henri, *Total Art: Environment, Happenings and Performance* (New York and Toronto: Oxford University Press, 1974), pp. 200-208; A. A. Bronson and Peggy Gale, eds., *Performance by Artists* (Toronto: Art Metropole, 1979) surveys recent performance art and supplies photographs, texts, and descriptions to document specific pieces; commentaries by various critics and authors are included, each with notes or a bibliography. *Performance by Artists* also contains a complete listing of articles, books, and catalogs published on performance art since 1969, pp. 304-18.

2. See also Richard Hayden Axsom, *Parade: Cubism as Theater* (Ph. D. diss., University of Michigan; Ann Arbor, Mich.: University Microfilms, 1975).

3. Lee Simonson, a leading American scene designer, organized an exhibition called *Theatre Art* for the Museum of Modern Art in 1934. The catalog—edited and introduced by her, published by W. W. Norton & Company, and with contributions by several other authors—presents a comprehensive history of stage design from the sixteenth century. A distinction was made between "art-artists" (easel painters) and artist-craftsmen (artists applying their work to the practical demands of theater). The exhibition concentrated on the latter.

4. For an extremely useful, extensively documented survey of artists' work for theater in the twentieth century see Henning Rischbieter, ed., *Art and the Stage in the 20th Century* (Greenwich, Conn.: New York Graphic Society, 1968). In an illuminating introductory essay, pp. 7-15, Rischbieter follows the development of the theater artist from Renaissance times. Janet Kardon offers an introductory view of contemporary collaborations in *Artists' Sets and Costumes*, exh. cat. (Philadelphia: Philadelphia College of Art, 1977).

1 Yale University drama students, *Model of a Naturalist Setting Designed by Donald Oenslager for a Scene from "Of Mice and Men" by John Steinbeck.*

The Stage Designs

In the past the roles of artist, architect, choreographer, stage designer, producer, and director were often united in one person, but today we distinguish the art of stage design from the fine arts. Working with some of the same elements of art as the painter or sculptor, the theater artist provides the visual aspects of a stage production. Despite multi-purposed beginnings, by the nineteenth century the theater artist had become a specialist, a stage designer who created costumes and settings befitting the time period of a particular play and answering the demands of the director. The stage designer's main concern was scene painting in the creation of wings, flats, and backdrops. But the use of perspective in painted scenery had reached a pinnacle in the eighteenth century, and later, this type of illusionism seemed lifeless and stale. So, with stock supplies of backdrops and costumes, theater artists became, by the end of the nineteenth century, even less than scene painters, "employed merely to repair, touch up, and complete existing scenery."[1]

Therefore, the emergence at the turn of the twentieth century of the vital stage designer once again having equal status with the director and playwright came as something of a revelation, particularly when the role of stage designer was handed over to leading easel painters of the day. Outdated and limiting, painted backdrops were abandoned in favor of naturalistic and complete stage settings incorporating real furniture, windows, and doors. This change was in part due to the role of certain enlightened producers like Duke George II of Saxe-Meiningen in Germany and André Antoine in France. It also reflected a general trend in the arts toward the natural depiction of contemporary life. Addressing literary and visual artists alike, Naturalist writers such as Emile Zola (1840-1902) advocated a close, scientific scrutiny of everyday life. Emphasis was placed on accuracy in the depiction of the overall environment, even in the tiniest detail. Followed precisely in terms of stage design, these ideas could result in the exact re-creation of real rooms on stage, or "Naturalism at its most pure, most uninspired and most dull. The illusion is complete, precisely because care has been taken to exclude any distinctive touch of design which would set this [room] apart from every other typical [room]."[2]

Antoine, at his Théâtre Libre (later Théâtre Antoine) in Paris; the celebrated Stanislavsky, who in 1898 opened the Moscow Art Theatre; and designers and producers in America recognized the need for stage settings which depended on actuality but which were balanced by "the element of distinctive design."[3] The study model reproducing Donald Oenslager's barn setting for John Steinbeck's *Of Mice and Men* [1][4] illustrates the effective use of simplified reality. An accumulation of a few appropriate details, such as the hay and pitchforks, evokes not only the natural look of a real barn but also mood and atmosphere.

The rebirth of aesthetic concern in stage design during the modern period placed new emphasis on the artist's role and personal vision. In France, both Antoine and his disciple, Aurélien Lugné-Poe,[5] recognized the contribution which could be made by painters; they engaged artists such as Pierre Bonnard, Edouard Vuillard, Henri de Toulouse-Lautrec, Maurice Denis, Edvard Munch, and others in the art of theater and program design. In Russia, a multimillionaire Muscovite, S. Mamontov, who built a theater for opera in 1888, "was probably the first person in Russia to decide that a stage setting should be something more than a background against which an actor, singer, or dancer moves. He felt that scenery could be used to provide a beautiful picture and to evoke a fitting sense of style and atmosphere. In order to obtain such scenery he turned to leading easel painters and gave them carte blanche."[6]

But the man most responsible for bringing about a revitalization of stage design was another Russian, Serge Diaghilev (1872-1929). His remarkable eye for the good and bad in art, his talent for synthesizing into a cohesive unity the disparate elements of stage production, his interest in the refreshingly new and different, and his willingness to take risks contributed to the huge success of his now-legendary Ballets Russes. Having at first patronized leading Russian painters and later the giants in the School of Paris—most notably Pablo Picasso, who put Cubism in motion with some of his costume designs for the ballet *Parade*, 1917—Diaghilev contributed as much to the visual arts as to the performing arts. Firmly committed to the concept of total theater in which choreography, music, libretto, and design were of equal importance, Diaghilev revealed his genius in the choice of collaborators.

Perhaps his deep understanding of the vital interaction among all the arts resulted from Diaghilev's background as an aesthete, an amateur of the arts. After some early musical training he had his beginnings in 1898 as the editor of an art review, *Mir iskusstra* (The World of Art, 1898-1904), which not only championed the new art movement of the same name in Russia but also helped to introduce in Russia new developments in art elsewhere in the world, particularly Impressionism, the Nabis, and post-Impressionism from France. Similarly, the exhibitions Diaghilev mounted in Europe early in the twentieth century created international interest in the bright, exotic works of such World of Art painters as Léon Bakst (1866-1924) and Alexandre Benois (1870-1960).

When Diaghilev decided to become a theater impresario and bring the Russian opera to Paris in 1908, and the next year to bring both the ballet and opera, he naturally turned to the World of Art painters to design sets and decor. Parisian audiences were overwhelmed by the amazing leaps of the dancer Nijinsky, the new music of the young composer Stravinsky, and the luxurious colors and imaginative freedom of Léon Bakst. From that point on, until Diaghilev's death in 1929, the Ballets Russes enjoyed virtually uninterrupted success and continued development, fostering through the war years the work of distinguished Russian painters and, after the war, providing a forum for the experimentation of Robert and Sonia Delauney; the Fauves Derain and Matisse; the Cubists Picasso, Braque, and Gris as well as a variety of other School of Paris and international artists.

Certainly, the model provided by Diaghilev's Ballets Russes early in the 1900s inspired similar collaborative efforts throughout the century. The remarkable thirty-year relationship, beginning in 1925, between modern dance pioneer Martha Graham and the Japanese-American sculptor Isamu Noguchi—which resulted in some twenty-two productions by Graham's company using sets, costumes, and props created by the sculptor—was characterized by a loosely defined and intuitive way of working together. Their similar temperaments and shared interest in simplicity, drama, myth, and psychology created a bond of mutual respect and the type of fully integrated visual dance theater developed by Diaghilev on a much grander scale. Merce Cunningham, with his vital patronage of contemporary American artists, such as Robert Rauschenberg and Jasper Johns, and his support of composers, such as John Cage and David Tudor, created an innovative dance company dedicated to Diaghilev's idea of total theater. Whereas the earlier impresario strove for full integration of art, choreography, libretto, and music, Cunningham cultivated the separate coexistence of the elements— "a disintegrated spectacle, in which the elements are independent of each other—and often are brought together only in the last stage of the creation." Considering the artistic freedom Cunningham gave the artists and composers who worked with him, critic Alexander Bland has said:

> Diaghilev would have loved Cunningham. Besides admiring him as an artist he would have respected the seriousness and discipline of his company, the spare wit and style of Rauschenberg's costumes and lighting, the consistent intervention of the choreography and the provocative strangeness of John Cage's musical accompaniments. Above all, his acute artistic antennae would have tingled at the sense that Cunningham was talking in the language of today.[7]

The language of Diaghilev's early Ballets Russes, while rooted in the folk and decorative tradition of his native Russia, spoke with the expressive power of brilliant color to the audiences of Paris. His leading designer then, Léon Bakst, was essentially a man of the theater who nonetheless approached the making of stage designs

2 Léon Bakst, *Design for a Stage Set*, 1915.

Hélène de Sparte"
au
Châtelet

Mme IDA RUBINSTEIN
dans le rôle d'Hélène

Aquarelle de
Léon BAKST

with the sensibilities of a painter. While his elaborate unidentified stage design in pencil [2] offers no evidence of the color for which he was famous, it does portray his flair for the exotic and his disregard for the dictates of Realism or Naturalism. A central dragon image with flame-like wings swoops down threateningly on a scene in which a king, backed up by an entourage, kneels before a fairy queen. The overall setting—with its turreted towers, a short bridge crossing a river (or perhaps a moat, in the foreground), and what appears to be a pageant wagon from which the queen steps down—suggests a medieval European town. Bakst's interest in the past culture of both Russia and his adopted France is balanced by an oriental flavor in this design, as in his other designs. The all-over intricate detailing of this flight into fantasy illustrates Bakst's study of Persian art and the panel paintings of early Italian and Flemish artists. The costume and frieze-like stance of the figure in a design for Ida Rubinstein as Helene, reproduced as an ad in the periodical *Comoedia Illustré* (Figure 1), indicate the strong influence of Greek and Roman art as well.

Natalie Gontcharova (1881-1962) and her lifelong companion Mihail Larionov (1881-1964) were among the Russian artists Diaghilev engaged who were not associated with the World of Art circle. Originally a student of sculpture, Gontcharova changed to painting in 1900 at the Moscow Institute of Painting, Sculpture, and Architecture. She was an exhibitor with the Golden Fleece movement in Russia, which stressed self-conscious nationalism, and like Bakst, she was inspired by native folkloric tradition. Inexpensive printed images (called *lubki*), toys, crude and brightly painted signboards, and

Figure 1. Léon Bakst, Russian, 1866-1924. *Hélène de Sparte*. Ca. 1920s. Page from *Comoedia Illustré* with reproduction of the water-color design. Lords Gallery, London.

stylized religious icons were aspects of Russian popular culture which fed Gontcharova's playful imagination. They inspired the creation of such colorful designs as the squid costume [3] or the headdress in the form of a fish [4], both made for the ballet *Sadko*—one act from Rimsky-Korsakov's opera *Le Royaume Sousmarin*— produced by Diaghilev in New York in 1916.[8] The royal blue and turquoise of the sleeveless dress for the squid costume are set off by the use of gold tissue, familiar in many Gontcharova costumes, here appliqued to the skirt in wavy vertical lines and covering the tall, wired cap with its fin-like projections and two large eyes of white silk and black sequins.

The same traditional and exotic impulses which shaped the art of Bakst and Gontcharova fed the creative sensibilities of two younger-generation, Russian-born American painters: Eugene Berman (1899-1972) and Simon Lissim (b. 1900). Neither artist worked for Diaghilev but they collaborated in dance and theater productions inspired by Diaghilev's concept of integrated theater. Simon Lissim, like Gontcharova and Bakst, grew up in Russia and spent many years in Paris before coming to New York in the 1940s. His *Yellow Sultan* [5], a gouache design of complex, mosaic-like detail; stylized, decorative flatness; and luxurious line and color recalls both Gontcharova and Bakst. In fact, the sultan subject— a common theme in Lissim's work—was painted in 1938 as a counterpart of Bakst's Sultanas from his famous designs for *Scheherazade*.[9]

Eugene Berman's costume study in ink for a female figure of 1945 [6] may have been for a proposed new version of *Concerto Barocco*— a ballet in one scene by George Balanchine with music by Bach, originally

3 Natalia Gontcharova, *Two-Piece Squid Costume for the Ballet "Sadko,"* ca. 1916.

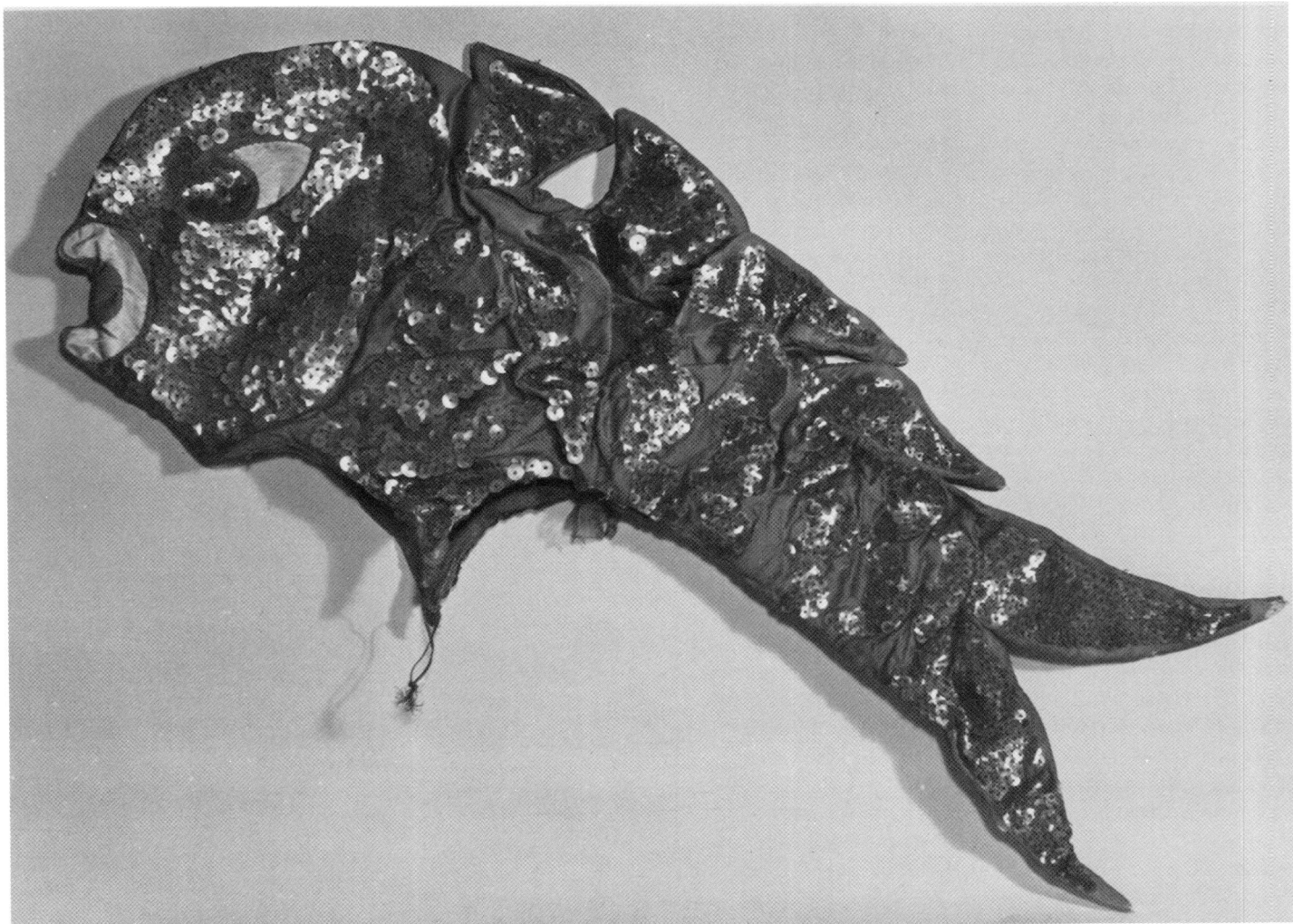

4   Natalia Gontcharova, *Fish Headdress for the Ballet "Sadko,"* ca. 1916.

5 Simon Lissim, *The Yellow Sultan*, 1939.

6 Eugene Berman, *Costume Study*, 1945.

performed in 1941 at Hunter College, New York, as part of Lincoln Kirstein's Ballet Caravan. Sketchy, diagonal-perspective lines converge quickly toward a vanishing point blocked by the woman's body seen from the back. The Baroque stylization of her classical dress is typical of Berman's other designs, and befits the title of the ballet. These aspects of Berman's work reflect a Western tradition of stage and costume design introduced by Renaissance artists in Italy and handled variously by English court masque artist Inigo Jones and his Italian contemporaries of the Baroque era, the Bibiena and Galliari families.[10]

In actuality, the works of Lissim and Berman and the works from which they derive (those of the Russian artists collaborating with Diaghilev's Ballets Russes) represent "the grand culmination of that same decorative style that had inspired designers of the Renaissance, the Baroque, the Romantic, and the Naturalist theatres."[11] By the 1920s ballet was conceived as a stunning spectacle designed to bewilder and overwhelm the spectator with grandiose visual and musical statements, at times impressionistic, but more often romantic and exotic. When she first worked for Diaghilev—by 1914— Gontcharova was considered a leading avant-garde artist in Russia with her cubistic movement called Rayonism. Even her more innovative and abstract designs, however, never fully broke away from the conventional form of stage settings as a painted surface.

If the majority of Diaghilev's productions were more or less traditional in terms of design, then the contribution Diaghilev made was to bring life back to a worn-out art form. Besides revitalizing ballet and nurturing music, he reintroduced the role of the creative, independent stage designer whose visual interpretation of libretto, music, or text became an integral part of the total production. His support and encouragement of the leading painters of his day demonstrated the reciprocal relationship between the performing and the plastic arts and pointed to many situations in which an artist's contributions to different fields can be inextricably linked.

Some of the most radical experiments in painting and sculpture, occurring in Europe during the first quarter of the twentieth century—for example, Futurism and Constructivism—were first tested in, or at least were found in, the realm of theater. The theories and creations of Futurist painter Enrico Prampolini (1894-1960) directly reflect the ideas of a leading innovator in Western theater: British theorist, designer, editor, and actor Edward Gordon Craig (1862-1966).[12] Craig and his Swiss counterpart, Adolphe Appia (1862-1928), called for the total reform of theater design through simplification and abstraction. To Appia a setting was not meant to dominate or even be fully integrated with the actor. Instead, Appia conceived of stage space as the domain of the actor, subordinated to him and used by him to reveal character and emotion. The model based on Appia's set for Gluck's *Iphigenia in Aulis* [7][13] reveals a series of stepped platforms stretching across the proscenium stage and backed by abstract block-like forms. All nonessential detail and the illusion of naturalistic space are gone. The set exists merely to amplify the movements and expressions of the actors. Gone, too, is the use of painted colors— so crucial to the total effect of Diaghilev's stage. Appia was the first designer to realize what the Impressionist and post-Impressionist painters already knew: "the importance of vibrating light in establishing the tactile value of forms and projecting them into space,"[14] as well as the expressive potential of colored light in creating mood and atmosphere. The balance and interaction of light, form, and space in Appia's theater were keyed, therefore, to the emotional tenor of the particular music or play.

Yale University drama students, *Model of an Abstract Setting Designed by Adolphe Appia for "Iphigenia in Aulis."*

8 Yale University drama students, *Model of an Abstract Setting Designed by Edward Gordon Craig.*

While at first glance the model of Craig's abstract stage set [8][15] designed around 1912 bears a remarkable resemblance to Appia's scene, after closer scrutiny, the essentially vertical orientation of Craig's rectangular columns is differentiated from the horizontal stress in Appia's definition of space. Simplified, basic forms arranged in space characterize the works of both designers; but in place of light, Craig emphasized movement in the creation of a truly vital, effective design. In a series of nineteen prints called *Scene* (of 1907) and in a set design for *Hamlet* (done in Moscow, 1912)—all of which resemble the model included here [8]—Craig developed a system of "screens." Walls made of canvas were moved into almost unlimited positions; cubes in the ceiling and floor were raised and lowered to varying

9 & 10　Edward Gordon Craig, *Design for a Stage Scene*, blocks executed 1900, printed in 1923.

Figure 2. Edward Gordon Craig, British, 1872-1966. *Design for a Headpiece*. Woodcut, 2 × 5⅝ inches (5 × 14.3 cm.); block executed 1908, printed 1923. The Cleveland Museum of Art, Gift of The Print Club of Cleveland. 24.335.

positions. Variety and mood would be provided by light, [16] an element which in some of Craig's designs, such as the woodcut print of 1900 [9], takes on a tangible quality.

Some of Craig's designs were intended for specific plays. One design (from 1900, signed in 1923) represents an outdoor scene with a white cloud-like formation dominating the center of the image. This woodcut [10] was reproduced in 1901 in *The Page*, a periodical edited by Craig, as a design for a scene in Handel's *Acis and Galatea*. However, the monumental scale of some of his landscape (Figure 2) or architectural designs prohibited production. If Craig argued that his designs were not scale drawings but rather suggestions of an effect an audience would receive, the fact remains that many of his sketches and prints were conceived not as designs for specific plays but as generalized statements, and as such, were often never constructed.

Craig's influence was as a theorist whose ideas were transmitted through designs and essays published in books, portfolios, and periodicals such as *The Page* or *The Mask*. The elemental, although convincing, nature of his and Appia's theories resulted in their continued use as the basis for design in both avant-garde and conventional theater. It is not surprising then that published in the January 1914 issue of Craig's *The Mask* was a manifesto written September 23, 1913, by a key proponent of Futurism—Marinetti—entitled "The Variety Theatre." Nor is it unlikely that, as a Futurist artist typically concerned with dynamism, Enrico Prampolini would reflect in his stage designs Craig's theories about movement and the art of theater.

If Craig was more the theoretician, then Prampolini was more the practitioner. Craig's screen system described above was never fully realized, but Prampolini, whose major emphasis was on scenery that would move, did integrate moving scenic elements with actors. Prampolini's set designs for *The Merchant of Hearts* suggest the progressive movement of hanging frames and screens and other parts such as the ladder-like extension in one design, shown here as it appeared in a series of commercial reproductions (Figure 3).[17] The silhouette of what appears to be an abstracted human figure hovers on the screen in many designs. While these experiments in dynamic scenography occurred relatively late in Futurist stagecraft (1927), they illustrate basic ways in which Futurist artists put their theories into practice. In their simplicity and abstractness, the individual designs are static, but viewed successively and as a group, they carry the potential for dynamic realization.

Figure 3. Enrico Prampolini, Italian, 1894-1956. *Set Design for "The Merchant of Hearts," Scene 1.* 1927. Reproduction. Special Collections Department, Northwestern University Library, Evanston, Illinois.

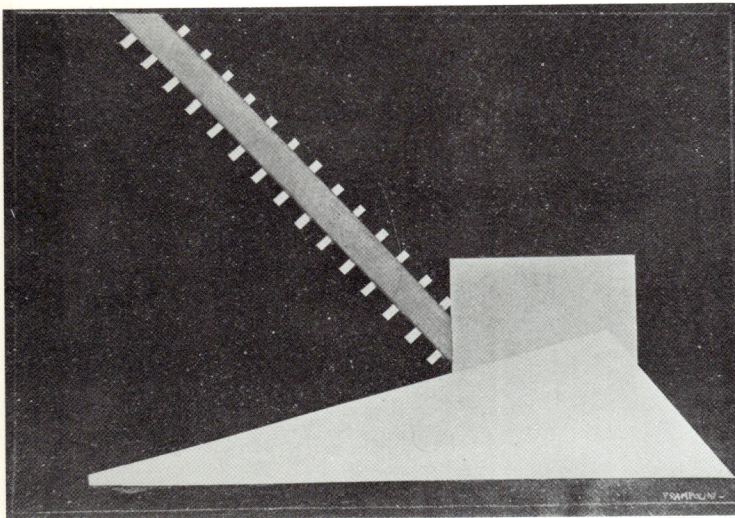

Yale University drama students, *Model of a Constructivist Setting Designed by Georgii Yakulov for "Girofle-Girofla" by Offenbach.*

Figure 4. Enrico Prampolini. *Mask Design for "Cocktail" by Marinetti*. 1927. Reproduction. Special Collections Department, Northwestern University Library, Evanston, Illinois.

Georgii Yakulov (1882-1928), a Russian avant-garde artist fond of the circus and other forms of popular entertainment, became active as a theater designer in 1918. His set for Offenbach's operetta *Girofle-Girofla*, 1922 [11], shown here in a study model,[18] consisted of simple, volumetric, multi-leveled spaces and was a practical, playful example of kinetic scenography. Constructing a "machine for actors" with a system of ladders, staircases, trap doors, and movable screens, Yakulov provided dynamic space and a total environment for the action of the play.

If Craig's, and subsequently Prampolini's or the Russian's, theories about kinetic stage sets had been strictly applied, a truly synthetic theater would have resulted, consisting of independently constructed set elements in constant motion to form visual and spatial relationships that were fluid and unlimited. Traditionally, the movements and expressions of actors, particularly in contrast to the static elements of the stage set, enlivened the space, thereby adding a dynamic element to stage performance. Yet with dominant, movable set pieces; with costumes designed to abstract and mechanize human form; and, even better, with the addition of large marionette-like figures capable of being suspended from the stage ceiling, the need for actors—whose individual characteristics and personalities could not be totally controlled (thus rendering the unity of the stage impure)—would be effectively eliminated.

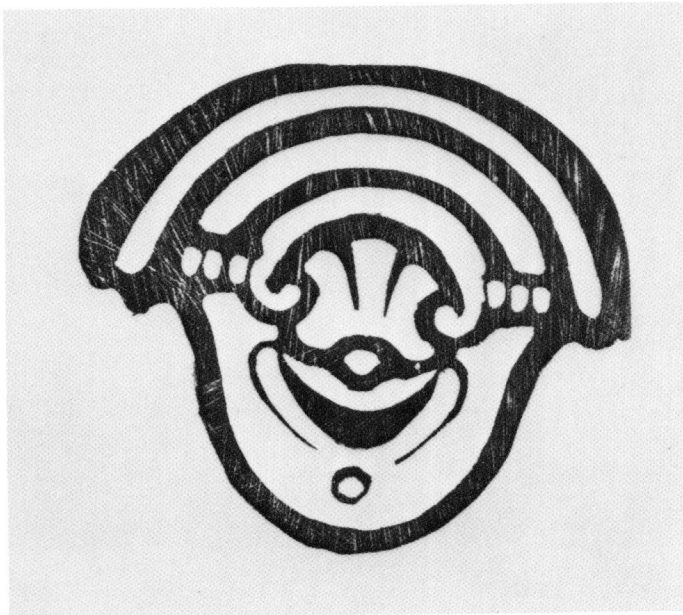

12 Edward Gordon Craig, *A Comic Mask*, block executed 1910, printed 1923.

Prampolini and other Futurists—for example, Giacomo Balla—did stage actorless performances.[19] But the fusion of performer and setting that Prampolini initially attempted was not unlike the total integration of figure and background in the Analytical Cubist paintings of Picasso, Braque, and others, and was the basis of Bauhaus theater in Germany as well as Russian theater at the time. This fusion, or synthesis, was accomplished through parallel abstraction in set and costume design and through dehumanization of the performer. The latter could be accomplished in several ways: through the use of masks composed of simple geometric shapes (Figure 4)—another feature borrowed from Craig's designs [12, 13]; through the use of non-naturalistic, patterned costumes; by choreographing mechanical, geometricized movements and postures for a performer who appears as a moving sculpture; and ultimately by incorporating non-human figurines, marionettes, or what Prampolini called actor-gases—"vibrations, luminous forms (produced by electric currents and colored gases) will wriggle and writhe dynamically, and these authentic actor-gases of an unknown theater will have to replace living actors."[20]

Alexandra Exter, a Russian painter and pioneer in avant-garde stage design was also concerned with movement. Her paintings were characterized by a dynamic use of color and abstract, sculptural form. These elements, evident in her costume designs for Oscar Wilde's *Salome* (Figure 5),[21] were attuned to the type of "synthetic" theater (in which scene design, lighting, and costuming were fused) advocated by Alexandr Tairov, who in 1914 founded the Kamerny Theatre in Moscow (where *Salome* was produced

13   Edward Gordon Craig, *Sketch for Headgear for "Hamlet,"* 1912.

Figure 5. Alexandra Exter, Russian, 1882-1949. *Costume Designs for "Salome" by Oscar Wilde*. 1917. Reproduction. Special Collections Department, Northwestern University Library, Evanston, Illinois.

in 1917). Exter and Tairov shared the goal of fully integrating moving performers into an environment or mood which was expressed through line, color, and mass. The costume designs for *Salome*, intended as part of a scenic whole, were conceived with the design for the set fully in mind: "massive columns and arrangements of steps in earth tones set against an abstract sky whose color changed to reflect the emotional atmosphere of the action."[22] Exter's subsequent experimentation with the rhythmic organization of space, which she viewed as a dynamic mechanism, was already evident in these early designs, culminating in her fully Constructivist theater of the 1920s.

The more radical solution to the problem of integrating moving performers, inanimate objects, and constructed space—a problem shared by Prampolini, Yakulov and Exter—involved the use of marionettes or other nonhuman performers. Once again Edward Gordon Craig's theories provided a point of departure: in 1908 he proposed that the performer be replaced by a nonhuman *Übermarionette* (Supermarionette). "Even though Prampolini added in *Futurist Scenography* that he also wanted to eliminate today's supermarionette recommended by recent reformers, his 'actor-gases' are nothing but a development and refinement of Craig's concept . . . ."[23] In fact, fed with a Futurist interest in the machine and modern technology, Prampolini designed, for *The Merchant of Hearts*, life-size marionettes representing the Sentimental Lady, the Primitive Lady, and the Mechanical Lady. Suspended from cords, the ladies, with movable parts not quite as numerous or flexible as those of traditional marionettes, performed with the live actors on stage. Exter's marionettes (composed of wood, various fabrics, metals, cardboard, plastic, glass, ribbons, wire mesh, and other "junk" materials) were small—about two feet tall—and were conceived not only as independent assemblages but also as integral parts of a stage production. Offering the designer the advantage of being able to change drastically the size and shape of the performer, the marionette brought to Futurism and Constructivism the means for total unification of a concept and its practical application in theater.

While Futurist performances may not be memorable in terms of realistic theater, in the opinion of at least one author, it "did have great influence on practically every nonrealistic approach to theatre," including that of the Dadaists, Surrealists, the French avant-garde in general; Pirandello in Italy; Wilder in the United States; and the Bauhaus in Germany.[24] The dehumanized, machine-like interpretation of character in Prampolini's designs and plays turns up in Germany with the uncharacteristic figurines that George Grosz (1893-1959) designed for Yvan Goll's *Methusalem*, 1922, a satire concerned with the ineptitudes of the eternal bourgeoisie. While never realized, Grosz's designs (represented here by a water-color drawing for the *Student* character [14]), offer a visual interpretation of Goll's ideas as expressed in the play and, like Exter's marionettes, call for the construction of figures from various pieces of junk. Pure form and design can express ideas, but the annotations on this and other designs heighten the impact of Grosz's sardonic wit (which was usually expressed visually with his more typical and direct style of draftsmanship and caricature): "Teeth like old piano keys," "Emits steam from time to time while speaking" (referring to the brain conceived as a partially exposed mechanical mess), "Here it can rattle and squeak while speaking," and (of the candle in the head), "Light of knowledge."[25] The

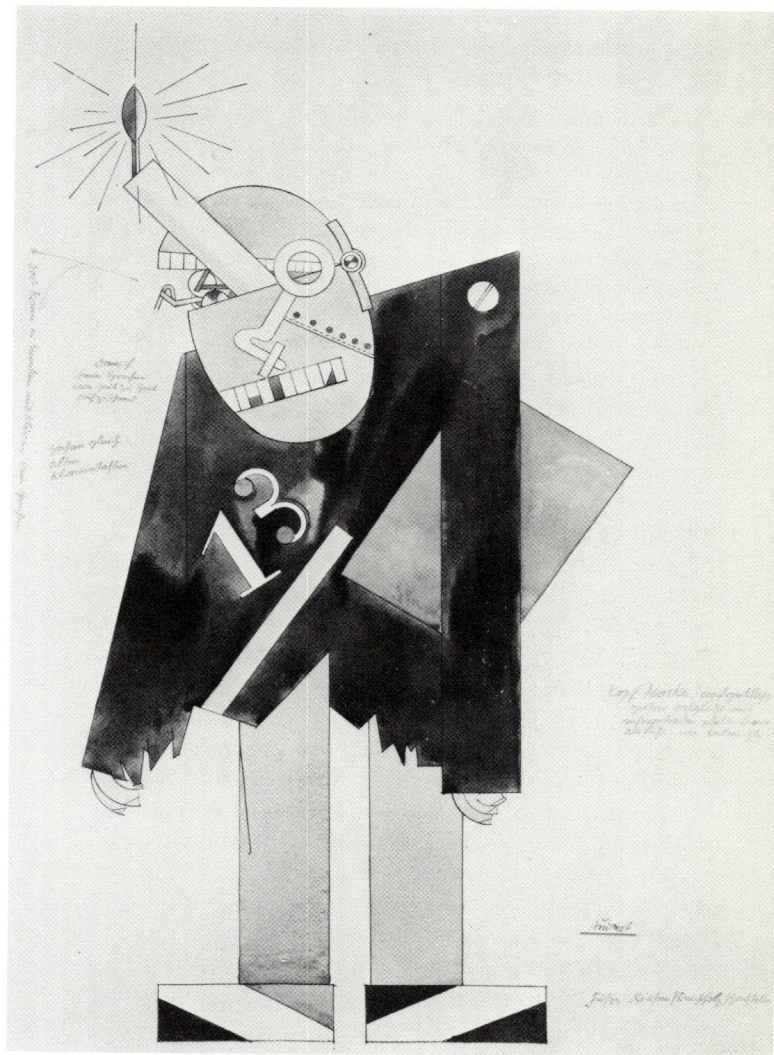

14 George Grosz, *Student: Design for Goll's "Methusalem,"* 1922.

guiding principle behind Grosz's mechanized and masked figurines, indeed behind the vast array of dehumanized, puppet-like characters designed for avant-garde theater in general, was stated by the playwright Goll himself:

> The new drama must have recourse to all the technological props which are contemporary equivalents of the ancient mask. Such props are, for instance, the phonograph which masks the voice, the denatured masks, and other accoutrements which proclaim the character in a crudely typifying manner: oversized ears, white eyes, stilts. These physiological exaggerations which we, shapers of the new drama, do not consider exaggerations, have their equivalents in the inner hyperboles of the plot....[26]

While not every painter is ultimately suited to the specific demands of stage design and production, painters' work for the stage in the twentieth century contributed not only to change in the history of stage design and the performing arts but also to the development of new concepts, movements, and styles in the visual arts as well. The transient nature of stage production offered to the painter or sculptor normally concerned with the creation of permanent images or objects a forum in which to test ideas. Futurism as a movement based in manifestoes and rhetorical outcry quite naturally took to the stage, and what could be a better way for an artist to explore the implied movement and visual dynamism of paintings and sculpture than to set the visual elements actually in motion on stage, as the Futurists, Constructivists, and so many other artists did? Even for those artists not as fully involved in the stage world, the designing of posters for theatrical productions or merely the observing of performers both on and off stage can have a profound effect on the artist's attempt to interpret the visual world.

1. Henning Rischbieter, ed., *Art and the Stage in the 20th Century: Painters and Sculptors Work for the Theater* (Greenwich, Conn.: New York Graphic Society, 1968), p. 8.

2. Bamber Gascoigne, *World Theatre: An Illustrated History* (Boston and Toronto: Little, Brown and Company, 1968), p. 269.

3. Ibid.

4. This model and the three others in the exhibition (cat. nos. 1, 7, 8, 11)—four of a group of eighteen—are accurate scale models which were built around 1940 for The Cleveland Museum of Art's extension exhibitions program by a group of graduate students in the drama department at Yale University. Under the direction of Dr. Elemer Nagy, who was formerly associated with Max Reinhardt in Vienna and who specialized in theater construction there and at Yale, the students used early prints and other documents to recreate outstanding examples of stage settings and architecture in the history of theater, ranging from the ancient Theater of Dionysus at Athens to modern scenes by Appia and Craig, and including representative settings in Chinese court theater and the Japanese Kabuki (popular theater). The eighteen models, plus one made in 1939 by Ernest Conklin of Roslyn, New York, of the Globe Theater as it was in Shakespeare's time, were originally purchased by the Museum with educational funds from a Rockefeller grant. On extended loan at Cleveland State University beginning in 1975, they were eventually purchased by the university's theatre arts area and are now on permanent display in the theatre arts building.

5. Aurélien Lugné-Poe, who met the artist Maurice Denis at the Lycée Condorcet, acted with the company of Théâtre Libre for two years, beginning in 1888 while he was studying at the Conservatoire de Musique et de Declamation. Lugné-Poe broke away from Antoine's naturalist Théâtre Libre and in 1893 founded his own symbolist and avant-garde Théâtre de l'Oeuvre. For an interesting discussion of Realism versus Symbolism in theater and its relationship to similar issues in the visual arts see Daryl R. Rubenstein, *The Avant-Garde in Theatre and Art: French Playbills of the 1890s*, exh. cat. (Washington, D.C.: Smithsonian Institution Traveling Exhibition Service, 1972).

6. Georges P. Annenkov, "Russian Painters and the Rebirth of Theatre Arts," in *Russian Stage and Costume Designs for the Ballet, Opera, and Theatre* (Washington, D.C.: International Exhibitions Foundation, 1967), p. 6.

7. Alexander Bland, *The Observer* [London], 2 August 1964, quoted in *Diaghilev/Cunningham* (Hempstead, N.Y.: The Emily Lowe Gallery of Hofstra University, April 16-May 26, 1974), unpaginated.

8. The original Ballets Russes production of *Sadko* (in Paris, 1911) utilized costumes and decor by Boris Anisfeld.

9. *Dreams in the Theatre: Designs of Simon Lissim*, exh. cat. (New York: The New York Public Library, Astor, Lenox and Tilden Foundations, 1975), p. 79.

10. For further information on Renaissance and Baroque stage design, see the following publications: (1) *Designs by Inigo Jones for Masques and Plays at Court* (Oxford: The University Press, 1924). Introduction and notes by Percy Simpson and C.F. Bell. (2) George R. Kernodle, *From Art to Theatre: Form and Convention in the Renaissance* (Chicago: University of Chicago Press, 1944). (3) Janus Scholz, ed., *Baroque and Romantic Stage Design* (New York: H. Bittner and Co., 1950). (4) Dunbar H. Ogden, *The Italian Baroque Stage* (Berkeley: University of California Press, 1978).

11. John E. Bowlt, *Stage Designs and the Russian Avant-garde* (Washington, D.C.: International Exhibitions Foundation, 1976), p. 5.

12. Michael Kirby, *Futurist Performance* (New York: E.P. Dutton & Co., 1971), p. 75. Kirby also suggests that Craig may have influenced not only Futurist scenography but also the basic theories of the movement. He points out that Craig's "monthly journal on the Art of the Theatre," *The Mask*, first published in 1908 in Florence, was internationally distributed and widely known. "It is probable," he concludes, "that Marinetti was aware of [Craig's] ideas when he wrote 'Foundation and Manifesto of Futurism' in 1909," the first document of Futurism.

13. See note 4.

14. Lee Simonson, "The Designer in the Theatre," in *Theatre Art*, exh. cat. (New York: W.W. Norton & Company for The Museum of Modern Art, 1934), p. 18.

15. See note 4.

16. See Denis Bablet, *Edward Gordon Craig* (New York: Theatre Arts Books, 1966), pp. 117–22.

17. The reproduction illustrated here was taken from a partial set of commercial theater–arts prints in an archival collection at Northwestern University Library, Special Collections Department, Evanston, Illinois. Little is known about this set of plates except that it was published in France. Signed and unsigned prints in limited and unlimited editions silk–screened or photo–mechanically reproduced were often made from artists' original painted or drawn stage designs. Some artists sold signed limited editions through reputable dealers or publishers to collectors. Other reproductions were incorporated into commercial sets which could be of value and interest to stage designers, students of stage production, or the enthusiastic theater–goer. In some cases, as with the reproductions at the Northwestern Library, the stage designs for a particular production were reproduced on a single plate with a photograph of the actual performance, thereby giving the viewer the opportunity to see the costumes or sets in use.

18. See note 4.

19. In 1917 Balla designed a set composed of volumetric movable elements lit from within for a short musical piece called *Fireworks*, composed by Igor Stravinsky in 1908, which was produced by Diaghilev's Ballets Russes at Teatro Constanzi in Rome, April 1917. Changing lights and moving-set configurations "performed" in time to Stravinsky's music. *Sacred Speed* was staged without actors by Prampolini in 1928. Other actorless performances staged by artists include the earliest example, *Victory Over the Sun*, produced by Russian suprematist Kasimir Malevich in December 1913 at "Luna Park" in Petersburg, and Alexander Calder's mobile set for Erik Satie's symphonic drama *Socrate*, which was sung by a man and woman but performed by suspended and rotating hoops, a red disc and a rectangular element. Originally produced by Virgil Thomson in 1936 at the Wadsworth Atheneum, Hartford, Connecticut, *Socrate* was revived in 1977 at the Beacon Theater, New York City, as part of a tribute to Calder on the eve of the first anniversary of his death. For more information see the publication cited in note 1 and Ruth Wolfe, "Calder's 'ballet without dancers,'" *Art News* 77 (February 1978), 108–10.

20. The elimination of actors was one aspect of the total reform of the stage that Enrico Prampolini advocated in a manifesto *Futurist Scenography* of April–May, 1915. This and other manifestoes plus playscripts by the Futurists were translated from the Italian by Victoria Nes Kirby and comprise the appendix in Michael Kirby's *Futurist Performance* (see note 12). Prampolini's discussion of actor–gases in *Futurist Scenography* appears on page 206.

21. This figure is taken from the same set of commercial reproductions which included Prampolini's designs; see note 17.

22. Alma H. Law, "The Revolution in the Russian Theater," *The Avant–garde in Russia, 1910–1930: New Perspectives*, exh. cat. (Los Angeles: Los Angeles County Museum of Art, 1980), p. 66.

23. Kirby, *Futurist Performance*, p. 105.

24. Ibid, p. 152.

25. Richard West translated the annotations in "Figure for Yvan Goll's *Methusalem*," *The Bulletin of The Cleveland Museum of Art* LV (April 1968), 92.

26. From Yvan Goll, "Superdrama," in *Anthology of German Expressionist Drama*, ed. and trans. Walter H. Soko (Garden City, N.Y.: Doubleday and Company, 1963), p. 11.

Figure 6. Detail of *Folies–Bergère, Fleur de Lotus* [17]. This stamp, affixed to the lower left portion of the poster, indicates that the appropriate tax was paid and that permission was granted to display the poster.

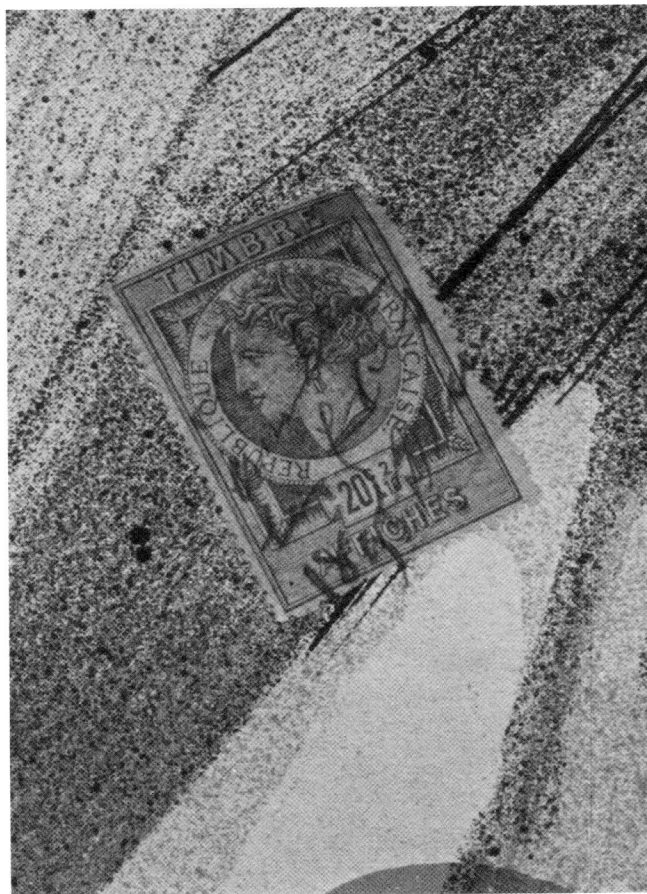

The Posters

A stage production—an opera, ballet, dramatic work, or music–hall song—depends on an audience for its ultimate motivation, and to insure a long and successful life. Expecting, quite naturally, to be entertained, a potential audience asks to be informed and enticed before committing time and expense to the viewing of a new production. Whether swayed by or impervious to the comments of critics and friends, the interested theater–goer still forms some prior opinion about a production based on the publicity it receives.

In the days before television and radio advertising, the poster served as the initial, and perhaps most effective, means of announcing a theatrical production. The responsibilities of the printed announcement were large: in a single visual statement—and in fierce competition with its neighbors on the street—the poster was expected to attract the attention of a passerby and, through its immediate impact, to evoke enough interest to encourage a visit to the theater. The poster fulfilled the dual purpose of imparting pertinent information and seducing the viewer with the names and faces of celebrities. In general, the more visible the image—in terms of size, color, and numbers posted—the more effective the poster would be.

The colorful commercial poster as we know it today is surprisingly youthful, however, within the history of advertising. While posters, bills, placards, or notices of one kind or another are "at least as old as the Egypt of Ptolemy,"[1] and although printed announcements were made possible by the invention and development of the printing press in the fifteenth century, it was not until the 1870s, when Jules Chéret (1836–1932) perfected his method of lithographic printing in successive colors, that the modern poster came into being.

Prior to Chéret's achievements, printmaking meant black and white; advertising emphasized primarily description and illustration. Chéret's work was timely, for the Industrial Revolution had not only made possible the means and technology for the faster, less expensive mass production of printed images, but it also resulted in a consumer–oriented economy based on the needs and demands of a growing middle class. In France, those individuals with more leisure time and greater financial acumen needed entertainment. From the romantic ballet at the beginning of the nineteenth century to the explosive emergence of avant–garde theater at the end of the century the performing arts flourished. Now, considering the range of possibilities for producing colorful, attractive prints, and with almost free access to public spaces for display (Figure 6),[2] more artists attempted printmaking: they recognized the popular audience as a viable one and they turned specifically to the design and production of posters. The poster format provided a creative outlet for the artist involved in individual experimentation with line or color. With Chéret paving a bright, colorful path, painters such as Toulouse–Lautrec, Pierre Bonnard, and Alphonse Mucha explored the visual possibilities of advertising and succeeded in capturing

the glamour and excitement of Parisian night life in their bold, vigorous designs. The marriage of aesthetic concerns and technical proficiency in the creation of posters during the final quarter of the nineteenth century expanded the limits of graphic art and led to significant changes in the whole psychology of advertising: the mere illustration and description of a product was deemed insufficient. Promotional announcements were further enhanced and newly charged with the "sensual appeal of color and design,"[3] and included the alluring images of women.[4]

Perhaps it was the temporal nature of the poster and of the theater itself which prompted a wide range of visual artists to design theatrical posters. The broad public exposure in the streets of Paris for limited spans of time offered the artists the kind of freedom that working for an individual private patron or for exhibition in the official Salons could not afford. Two of the leading graphic designers during the last two decades of the nineteenth century both launched their careers with poster designs for theatrical productions. Both Jules Chéret and Alphonse Mucha began long involvements with the stage world by producing posters for Sarah Bernhardt (1845–1923)—one of the leading actresses of the day as well as the manager/director of a number of theaters in Paris, most notably the Théâtre de la Renaissance during the years from 1893 to 1898.[5]

Jules Chéret's thirty–year command over Parisian advertising began in 1866 with a poster announcing a performance by the young Bernhardt. Born in Paris in 1836, Chéret was apprenticed at age 13 for three years to a commercial lithographer. He gained further

16   Jules Chéret, *Olympia*, 1892.

experience with other lithographers, and after a six–month stint in London he returned to Paris in 1858, where he did a poster design for Offenbach's operetta *Orphée aux enfers*. Despite the success of the poster, he received no further commissions and so returned to London, where he produced designs for the products of the perfume manufacturer Eugène Rimmel. Sponsored by Rimmel, Chéret returned once again—in 1866—to Paris and established a print shop for lithography.

By 1869 Chéret had nearly perfected his method of color lithographic printing from successive stones. The superimposed impressions were each inked in a different color, with the first plate setting down a black outline. The next plate added a vibrant red which was softened by the third plate supplying a gradated background that ranged from cool tones (blues or greens) at top to warm tones (yellow or orange) at the bottom. The brilliant reds and greens of the early posters were expanded to include more yellow, blue, and orange in later works. In general, Chéret's colors gradually grew lighter, more sophisticated, and imbued with the air of gaiety which characterized La Belle Epoque. In addition, the spattering, stippling techniques he used and his method of blending transparent inks both softened the mechanical edge of the printing process and added texture and depth.[6] Many adored the bright, festive air of Chéret's works.

Perhaps the real key to his success and popularity was due not only to the new emphasis on color in his work but also to the energetic portrayal of the music halls and theaters of Paris. In both color and theatricality Chéret paid tribute to the lively images of

17   Jules Chéret, *Folies-Bergère, Fleur de Lotus*, 1893.

Watteau and Tiepolo, masters of the preceding century who were then greatly admired. His graphics were bold, convincing, and clean; his skill in composing figures and words into a mutually complementary design, as in the lively music–hall scene of *Olympia* [16], attracted even the most casual passersby. The *Olympia* poster of 1892 and the *Fleur de Lotus* poster for the Folies Bergère [17] revealed the large format and the free quality of Chéret's poster designs from the 1880s on. The composition in each poster opens widely, like the dancers' arms. The drawn black lines of early posters are here replaced by blue ones, and the gradated background, once standard for his designs, is completely gone. Chéret's posters shimmered like the paintings of Turner—another master he greatly admired—and like the butterflies and mother-of-pearl specimens he kept in his studio.

By 1890 the extremely prolific Chéret was celebrated throughout Europe, America, and Australia. His posters covered the walls of Paris and captured the frolicking atmosphere of the theaters and cabarets, virtually bringing that atmosphere out into the streets for everyone to enjoy.

On the first day of 1895—as if to announce a new beginning—a very different-looking poster appeared on the streets to almost instant public praise and enthusiasm. *La Revue Illustré* spoke of the poster for Sarah Bernhardt's production of *Gismonda* by Sardou at the Théâtre de la Renaissance as "this white window, this mosaic on the wall" and extolled its creator, Alphonse Mucha (1860–1939), as an artist worthy of succeeding Chéret.[7] The immediate critical and public success of Mucha's *Gismonda* overwhelmed the young artist who, despite a natural drawing ability and eight years in Paris working as an illustrator, was relatively unknown and barely making a living. While his initial training in art was as a scene painter for the leading firm of theatrical scenery and curtain design in Vienna, and although later in Paris he received a regular income from the periodical *Costume au Théâtre* for which he recorded the details of new productions, he had not designed a poster—let alone one for the theater—before *Gismonda*.

The story of this fateful assignment is much celebrated. When Miss Bernhardt telephoned the print shop Lemercier close to Christmas Eve in 1894, Mucha had no idea that this would be the long-awaited opportunity to propel his career as well as the beginning of a close association with the famous actress. Bernhardt desperately needed a poster, and the disgruntled shop manager de Brunhoff turned to Mucha, who happened to be in the shop correcting prints. Mucha agreed to do a design, having to borrow the appropriate hat and tailcoat in order to visit the fashionable theater to meet with his new client. Mucha's original sketch for the *Gismonda* poster was worked out on a marble table surface in a nearby café. The disapproving de Brunhoff and Lemercier only reluctantly allowed Mucha to submit the tempera painting he had worked up. Not only was Miss Bernhardt delighted with the design, but she immediately contracted Mucha for six years to design posters as well as costumes and scenery for her productions. For Sarah, the Byzantine element of Mucha's design—the mosaic effect in the frieze and tympanum crowning her head—captured the flavor of the play while feeding the fashionable taste among the cultural audiences of the day for Byzantine associations.[8] In addition, the intricacies of the heavily embroidered robe she wears in the poster, the overall vertical design of the poster (a format Mucha favored in most of the posters which followed), and most important, the elongated elegance and tragic air of her image pleased her greatly. For the first time, Miss Bernhardt felt she had found an artist who could go beyond physical appearance and surface decoration, and with every inch of his all-over design, could not only visualize the essence of the dramatic work but also express the varied moods and character of her stage presence and personality.[9]

In all, Mucha designed nine posters for Sarah Bernhardt between 1895 and 1900 of which two are included here: *La Samaritaine*, 1897 [18], and *Lorenzaccio*, 1899 [19]. His work for her "placed him in the front rank of contemporary decorative art."[10] Theirs was a relationship built on mutual support and admiration. The designs he executed for Bernhardt went beyond the realm of theater work: he created jewelry, hairstyles, and clothing for her as well. He was her friend and confidant, and to him, she represented the ideal woman. As his son Jiri Mucha pointed out, "Bernhardt occupied a unique position in my father's life, her patronage had been the instruments of his success, her plays provided a showcase for his designs," and, it was "the force of her personality" which encouraged him and offered him an unending source of creative inspiration.[11]

When Mucha's graphic style emerged with assurance by 1895, it captured the eyes and hearts of Parisians despite the subtlety, the subdued tones, and the conspicuous lack of red—quite different from the boisterous images of Chéret. The hallmarks of Mucha posters—the sinuous lines; accentuated contours; attenuated figures; long, spiraling tresses

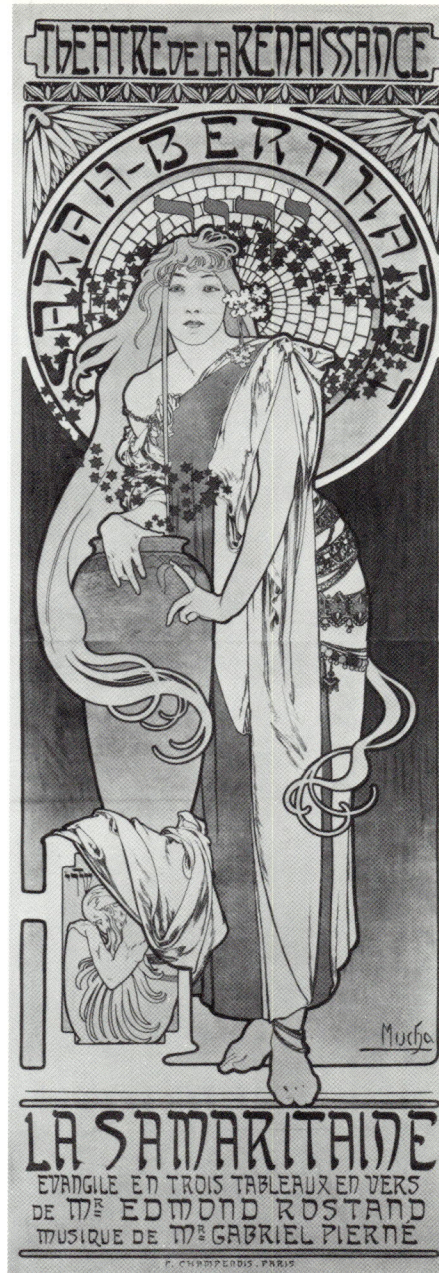

18 Alphonse Maria Mucha, *La Samaritaine*, 1897.

of luxurious hair; intricate surface patterns comprised of signs and symbols of a variety of sources, ranging from the traditions of folk-decoration in his native Czechoslovakia to the world of the occult—all would later form the definitive example of Art Nouveau graphic design. Ironically, Mucha denied this term altogether, stating that "art is eternal, it cannot be new,"[12] and eschewed associations with any one particular style or group of artists.

Yet, Mucha's success in the realm of advertising and the reason his posters were avidly collected as soon as they appeared on the streets depended on more than the sensual appeal of line or a style currently in vogue. The one factor that Mucha and Chéret had in common was perhaps the same factor that accounted for their individual popularity despite the disparities in their visual approaches: both Mucha and Chéret celebrated the aesthetic of woman, each sharing with a voracious public a unique conception of feminine beauty. Chéret captured the verve and alluring energy of Parisian dancers and entertainers such as Charlotte Wiehr, the slender, red-headed Danish dancer who was his favorite model.[13] "La Cherette," as she was nicknamed, can be seen as a forerunner of the American "Gibson Girl," who, likewise, proved the appeal of glamour and the selling powers of good looks and a vivacious personality. Sarah Bernhardt, as Mucha's quintessential woman, embodied mystery and elegant grace in such images as the *Lorenzaccio* poster [19], and suggested strength balanced by vulnerability in *La Samaritaine* [18]. Although based on the intimate observation of a few models and, particularly, of one of the world's

19 Alphonse Maria Mucha, *Lorenzaccio*, 1899.

best-loved celebrities, Mucha's posters ultimately expressed the universal appeal of all women. In focusing on the female image, Chéret and Mucha were doing what so many artists had done before; but now, despite the stylization, their women were real—not the goddesses or heroines of mythology and literature—and they were accessible to everyone due to the simple fact that poster images, as a commercial art, were in the public domain.

Even when raised to the level of fine art, as it was in the hands of Mucha or Chéret or the Italian-born artist Emanuel-Joseph-Raphael Orazi (1860–1934) [20], the theatrical poster and the world it advertised remained within reach: the collector of modest means could afford to buy these color lithographs (the less honorable could steal them, and often did) and, for a few francs, the average person on the street could enter the theater or *café-concert* and actually see, in person, the divine Sarah, la petite Cherette, and the rest of the cast of characters. Beyond its primary function of announcing a new production, the theatrical poster preserved the aura of the production and its brightest stars.

20 Emanuel-Joseph-Raphael Orazi, *Palais de la Danse*.

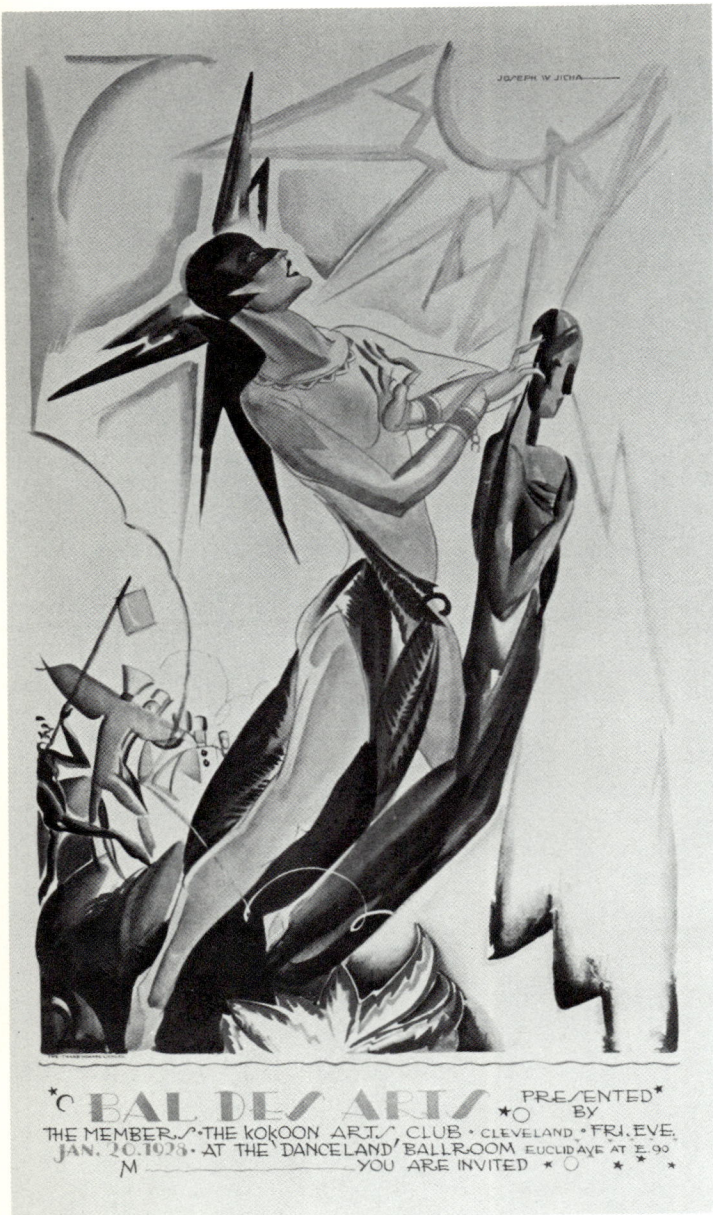

BAL DES ARTS **PRESENTED** BY
THE MEMBERS THE KOKOON ARTS CLUB · CLEVELAND · FRI. EVE.
JAN. 20.1928 · AT THE 'DANCELAND' BALLROOM EUCLID AVE AT E 90
M   YOU ARE INVITED * O * * *

1. According to James Laver writing about "Theatrical Posters" in *The Oxford Companion to the Theatre*, 3rd ed. (London: Oxford University Press, 1972), a papyrus dated ca. 150 BC contains information about two slaves who escaped from the neighborhood of Alexandria.
2. A law passed in France July 9, 1881, allowed (with payment of the appropriate tax) the placement of posters anywhere except on churches, voting rooms, and areas reserved for official notices. For further information see Phillip Dennis Cate, *The Color Revolution: Color Lithography in France 1890–1900*, exh. cat. (Rutgers, N. J.: The State of New Jersey, Rutgers University Art Gallery, 1978), p. 10.
3. Ibid., p. VIII.
4. For a discussion of this theme see Gabriel P. Weisberg, *Images of Women: Printmakers in France from 1830–1930*, exh. cat. (Salt Lake City: Utah Museum of Fine Arts, 1978).
5. Nicole Wild, ed., *Les arts du spectacle en France: affiches illustrées (1850–1950)*, Catalogues de la Bibliothèque de l'Opéra, II (Paris: Bibliothèque Nationale, 1976), 190.
6. A description of the method Chéret practiced in lithographic printing throughout the 1870s and early in the 1880s was offered by Henri Beraldi in 1886 in *Les graveurs du XIX siècle*, vol. I, and reprinted in Cate, *The Color Revolution*, pp. 3–4.
7. Quoted by Jiri Mucha et al., *Alphonse Mucha: Posters and Photographs* (New York: St. Martin's Press, 1971), p. 12.
8. Brian Reade, *Art Nouveau and Alphonse Mucha* (London: Her Majesty's Stationery Office, 1967), p. 4.
9. Mucha et al., *Alphonse Mucha*, p. 12. Prior to Mucha, Sarah Bernhardt commissioned other artists to design posters, but each was a one-time-only assignment.
10. From a review in *Christian Science Monitor*, January 31, 1921, on the occasion of an exhibition at The Brooklyn Museum of Mucha's nationalistic murals for his native country, Czechoslovakia.
11. Mucha et al., *Alphonse Mucha*, p. 19.
12. Ibid., p. 37.
13. Jane Abdy, *Posters by Jules Chéret*, exh. cat. (London: The Ferrers Gallery, 1967), p. 8.

21 Joseph W. Jicha, *Kokoon Arts Club, Bal des Arts—Poster/Invitation*, 1928.

The Players

Posters brought modern European and American audiences into theaters, music halls, and *café-concerts*. Of course, not all performers encountered within were well known or even recognized. The colorfully portrayed visages of the stars may have populated the streets, but the anonymous faces of the *corps de ballet* or the *troupe de théâtre* filled the stage behind and around the center spotlight. While European performers of all talents and levels of fame or notoriety have captured the attention of the visual artists from the Baroque era through the nineteenth century, the most famous were more often portrayed, and their resultant images generally fall into two categories: conventional portraits and documentary prints.[1]

In the conventional portrait, leading actors and actresses—like heroes, kings, and queens—are notable sitters before the painter's, not the critic's, scrutiny. To the artist's audience, the performer when posed formally was not the character in a play, but rather was the distinguished gentleman or elegant lady, who might be fashionably dressed as the actress Sarah Siddons was before the eyes of a leading portraitist of eighteenth-century England, Thomas Gainsborough (1727-1788) (Figure 7).

Figure 7. Thomas Gainsborough, English, 1727-1788. *Mrs. Siddons*. Black chalk, 18⁵⁄₁₆ × 13⁷⁄₈ inches (46.6 × 35.3 cm.). The Cleveland Museum of Art, John L. Severance Fund. 76.6.

The documentary prints of theatrical personalities preserve the celebrity not merely as a stylish person but also in the dress and attitude of a current or famous role. Edward Gordon Craig (1872-1966) frequently portrayed his illustrious godfather, the actor Sir Henry Irving (1838-1905), both in and out of theatrical roles. The woodcut portrait of *Henry Irving as "Badger"* [22] exemplifies Craig's style in portraiture as well as in innovative scene designs. It minimized detail, contrasted solid black and vast areas of white, and employed a strong line which, in places, asserted itself as an independent abstract shape within a total composition. Despite the economy of this and most of his portraits of Irving, Craig conveyed the sense of a theatrical character balanced with and ignited by the presence of a dynamic actor. This image could stand as a visual interpretation of a statement about Irving made by his leading lady of more than twenty years, Ellen Terry, Craig's mother: "He was quiet, patient, tolerant, impersonal, gentle, close, crafty, incapable of caring for anything outside his work."[2] Perhaps the intimacy with which Craig approached his subjects, and the fact that his life was filled with theater—with the writing about it, the acting, the designing, and the numerous relatives and friends involved in it—account for the effectiveness of *Henry Irving Ellen Terry: A Book of Portraits* (1899), a set of nineteen wood engravings embodying the very essence of a Hamlet or Ophelia, the strength and skill of Sir Henry and Miss Terry, and also the commitment and personal vision of Craig himself. This vision and the ability to isolate essential detail characterize the portrait of Irving as Fielding's Badger from "Don Quixote in England," an

22 Edward Gordon Craig, *Henry Irving as "Badger,"* block executed 1900, printed 1924.

image intended for publication in Craig's periodical *The Page*. If the portraits bore evidence of Craig's inextricable tie with the stage world—with the personalities and characters that populated Craig's theater and life—then for Craig who began a career as an actor (Figure 8), the periodical was like a stage:

Being an actor, though now no longer acting, the need for appearing before the public was still curiously strong in me. Had I been training as a painter, or in any art or craft, I should certainly not have come out prematurely in any publication like *The Page*. But being actor-trained, I could only do my bit on a public stage—a curtain had to rise at a certain hour on a certain date, to rouse me. This curtain rising was the first number of *The Page*. Only a few copies were printed, and fewer were sold. I worked hard at its creation—many wood-cuts, slight text. It appeared from 1898 to 1901—it cost next to nothing—only life.[3]

Figure 8. Photograph of Edward Gordon Craig in a scene from *Cymbelline* at the Lyceum Theatre in London, September 22, 1896. Courtesy Special Collections Department, Northwestern University Library, Evanston, Illinois.

And for the writer-editor-designer-critic Craig who emerged and developed in the periodicals, books, and portfolios, *The Page* also served as a forum:

> *The Page*, slight as it was, was helped by contributions of work generously given to it by Will Rothenstein; a Coquelin drawing; something by Charles Conder (through Will R.); by J. J. Guthrie; by James Pryde; a unique sketch by Irving, an original MS. of Whitman; two pen sketches by Bastien-Lepage—of H. I. and Sarah Bernhardt; a drawing by Burne-Jones; a caricature of Will Rothenstein by Max Beerbohm; a caricature of Max by Will R.; music by Martin Shaw, by Joseph Moorat and by Sir A. C. Mackenzie; verse or prose by Miss L. Alma-Tadema and Oliver Madox Hueffer, brother of Ford Madox Ford.[4]

The image of Irving as Badger, wearing a tall hat from which close striations meander down along the collar of his coat and beyond, is as much decorative as it is documentary. The sparse lines which define character in the Irving/Badger face are continuous; the linear arabesque of smoke billowing from Irving's pipe fills the upper portion of the print and trails down along the left edge. But the real strength of this image and Craig's style lies in the remarkable balance between portraiture, characterization, and decorative design.

23 William Nicholson, *Sarah Bernhardt*, 1964.

24 James Abbott McNeill Whistler, *The Dancer, No. 1 (Connie Gilchrist)*.

In traditional theatrical portraits, either a celebrity-personality or a character role dominate the image. In the case of the latter, whether or not the character is met on stage and is with other players or alone, it is the visual documentation of the production or the celebration of a memorable portrayal by an acknowledged star that initiates the image. Irving as Badger or Sarah Bernhardt as herself in William Nicholson's woodcut [23] transcend the temporal quality of a single performance. These portraits serve as timeless reminders of the life or career, indeed, the very aura of a star.

The American artist living in England, James Abbott McNeill Whistler (1834-1903), rarely turned to theater or portraiture in his paintings or prints. Yet, his tiny ink drawing *The Dancer, No.1*, an image possibly of Connie Gilchrist [24], not only reveals the small scale of his many images drawn from a keen observation of life and activity around him but also shows his tendency to transform the visual stimulus of life into an aesthetic statement. The drawing is less the celebrated dancer on stage (or even the anonymous performer) than it is the sum total of rapidly scratched lines and cross-hatches which coalesce in the form of a young woman who wears a transparent veil-like gown which she holds open like the butterfly of Whistler's insigina.[5] With raised arms, a partially opened fan in her left hand, a right leg extended in front and bent at the knee, the woman dances in a timeless moment in indefinable space. Her movement is suggested by energized lines which also convey a sense of the actual performance, even though audience and stage are not visible.

Connie Gilchrist (1865-1946) was an English actress who began her career as a child in pantomine and later became a skipping-rope dancer. She became a hit in a comic role in 1880, yet this "lovely woman" preferred burlesque to straight comedy in a brief but successful career which ended when she became Countess of Orkney in the late 1880s. It is quite likely that Whistler saw Connie Gilchrist in London and made sketches either during or after the performance. It is also possible that the dancer is Loie Fuller (1862-1928), who was known for her flowing, transparent costumes—like the one depicted in *The Dancer, No. 1*. Whistler was in Paris during her highly successful, premiere cabaret season in 1892/93 and is known to have sketched her.[6] Yet, in his drawing, the identity of the dancer—indeed the subject of the dance itself—is less important than the formal aspects of the image. In the exhibition catalog *The Stamp of Whistler* Robert Getscher discusses Whistler's concern with the primacy of formal elements: "As [Whistler] wrote of his painting *Harmony in Grey and Gold*, a snow scene with a single black figure and a lighted tavern: 'I care nothing for the past, present, or future of the black figure, placed there because the black was wanted at that spot. All that I know is that my combination of grey and gold is the basis of the picture.' "[7]

Like Whistler, Edgar Degas (1834-1917) concentrated on realizing the pictorial potential of the dancer's moment on stage. However, dance—more specifically, ballet—was a deliberate focus for Degas rather than an incidental subject as it was for Whistler. Degas studied dance closely, from various viewpoints—from the audience and from backstage, in the rehearsal halls and in practice studios. He presents more than the supreme on-stage performance: he brings us the offstage scenes and private moments of the dancers' world to which he was privy. Thus we capture a glimpse of *Ballet Girls* [25] standing about, adjusting costumes, and stretching offstage either in the wings during a performance or in the rehearsal hall.

Furthermore, the players in Degas's stage world were not usually the celebrities. They did not carry with them the aura of fame or the glamor of stardom; instead, they attest to the real experience of hard work and the unwavering discipline demanded from all dancers in the art of classical ballet. Degas quickly and yet empathetically sketched the young *Ballet Dancer* [26] in a moment of rest from grueling daily exercises and endless lessons. The dancer is seated on a low bench; her head lies heavily in her right hand, and her elbow meets a raised, bent right knee. Degas recognized that the work involved in the day-to-day training and the constant struggle toward a point of perfection in the dancer's world matched his own efforts to master drawing and the art of painting. "He discovered that just as he has to draw each day, repeating and correcting scores of times, observing ceaselessly, remembering gestures, tones, masses and changes of light, so the dancer must discipline herself and like him, without becoming mechanical ... daily, in the heat or cold, whether physically inclined or not, she must work for hours ... until technique, becoming so perfected, no longer requires conscious thought and all can then be given to artistry."[8]

Even while noting the weary physical status of the resting dancer, Degas transformed her attitude of fatigue into an elegant, almost abstract, design. The head, bodice, and left leg are the most clearly defined elements, but Degas perceives the dancer as a self-contained form composed of a series of discrete lines and shapes all deferring to an overriding and unifying curve which sweeps gracefully from the head of the dancer all the way to her left foot.

25 Hilaire Germain Edgar Degas, *Ballet Girls.*

Degas's ultimate concern with form and movement explains the anonymity of his dancers. There are few, if any, celebrities in his theatrical works, and only in several cases is a specific ballet identifiable.[9] The players onstage or in the wings are seen at oblique angles or from behind [25]. Partial views, figures fragmented by poles or the edge of scenery flats, and groups of dancers crowded into shallow foreground space offer a casual snapshot rendition and suggest close though detached observation of the real scene. Even though Degas's love was the classical ballet that had flourished in France during the first half of the nineteenth century, Theodore Reff notes: "The ballets Degas saw at the opera of his day were rarely classical in content; but despite their exotic and folkloric subjects and settings, he invariably showed the dancers in their traditional white *tutus*, which had been introduced in the neoclassical period."[10]

Perhaps there were no stars in Degas's stage world simply because by the time he began his celebrated involvement with theatrical subject matter, in the 1870s, French ballet had become stale and uninspired and all the great classical ballet dancers of the Romantic epoch were retired, some from the stage forever.[11] "The scene had changed indeed, from the Opéra to the Folies-Bergère, the Jardin de Paris, and the Moulin Rouge; the idols of the Parisian *galants* were no longer the stars of the classical ballet, but Loie Fuller, Eglantine, Jane-Avril, and La Goulue."[12]

While Degas was the objective, informed observer of ballet, taking care to depict correctly the dancers' standard repertoire of positions, he was more the student of movement and perfected form and less the chronicler of the contemporary stage than was Henri de Toulouse-Lautrec (1864-1901), one of his strongest admirers. Both men were born into relatively well-to-do

26 Hilaire Germain Edgar Degas, *Ballet Dancer.*

Degas

families for which a typical education included at least exposure to serious theater, opera, and ballet. Toulouse-Lautrec's paintings, posters, and lithographs reflect this background: they offer a range of theatrical subjects, from the dramatic classical Opéra or the lighter Comédie Française to the advant-garde Théâtre Libre and the Symbolist Théâtre l'Oeuvre. While Toulouse-Lautrec may have spotlighted the leading actors and actresses of serious theater during the 1890s—including Sarah Bernhardt, whom he presented in a scene from Racine's *Phèdre*—his overall productions featured the faces and feel of the *café-concerts*. This was a world he chose to study and then came to live in. Like Degas, he was the artist-observer; moreover, he became the knowing participant whose skill lay in pinpointing the salient characteristics of the places he frequented and the persons he knew. His mastery over subject matter, emotional content, and visual structuring in the making of a picture reaffirmed itself with each candid portrayal of popular stars and familiar entertainment settings. He identified personally with the actors, singers, dancers, entertainers, and, most poignantly, the clowns— each of whom "could stand as equivalent to the derided, unrecognized artist."[13] Most assuredly Toulouse-Lautrec succeeded in conveying, through specifics, the full ambience and character of night life in modern Paris during the lively 1890s.

One of the most talked-about performers of the day was the American Loie Fuller (1862-1928), who took Paris by storm at the Folies-Bèrgere during the 1892/93 season. Her singular approach to stage performance was based on an interest in lighting effects. Inspired by the

27 Henri de Toulouse-Lautrec, *Miss Loie Fuller*, 1893.

sensation of light, color, and organic forms in nature, she created a repertoire of dances the look and names of which evoked, and on occasion motivated, the imagery and motifs of the enormously popular Art Nouveau. As a style in the decorative and graphic arts as well as painting, Art Nouveau placed the emphasis on the decorative effect of swirling lines, flat color, and stylized forms from nature as evidenced in Loie Fuller's Serpentine Dance, Fire Dance, Butterfly Dance, White Dance, or others. Toulouse-Lautrec's lithographic tribute [27] to this sensational performer, who considered herself an instrument of light, capitalizes on the visual effects of her trademark: the billowing folds of a long gown manipulated (while she stood still) by sticks held in each hand underneath her gown. The large expanse of color in the print rushes upward and glows against the dark, spattered, indistinct background like the effects of smoke and fire she tried to capture with costume, movement, and colored lights projected through a square of glass built into the stage floor in Fire Dance, the piece which inspired the artist.[14]

Toulouse-Lautrec's ability to isolate and exaggerate to just the right degree certain elements—the artificial trappings of a performer's costume or salient physical features—resulted in memorable images which come close to caricature in their immediacy; simplicity; and teasing, affectionate wit. With a few simple lines Toulouse-Lautrec evokes the figure and style of the well-liked *diseuse* Yvette Guilbert (1867-1944) [28,29]. (In a similar way Betty Rubinstein captures the essence of Isadora Duncan with a minimum of lines and details in an ink drawing [31].) Guilbert's practice of reciting

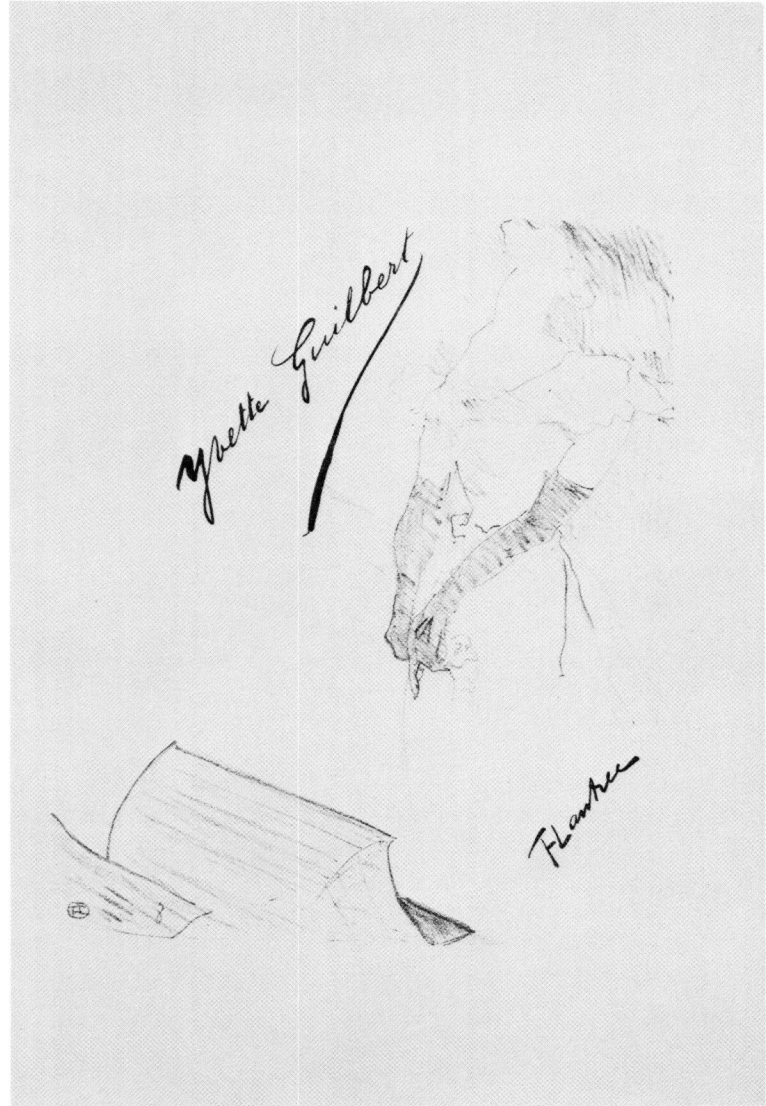

28   Henri de Toulouse-Lautrec, *Yvette Guilbert*, 1898.

29 Henri de Toulouse-Lautrec, *Yvette Guilbert: On Stage*, 1898.

30 Henri de Toulouse-Lautrec, *May Belfort*, 1895.

rather than singing the songs written specifically for her won her, at first, the skepticism and then the unwavering devotion of those in her audience, including Lautrec. Her standard attire featured a low-cut dress which accentuated her slim figure, and long black gloves—so familiar that when they were depicted separately by Lautrec as the cover image for an album of lithographic prints he devoted to Guilbert, they brought her instantly to mind.

Beyond the concern with the truthful, if not completely objective, rendering of totally familiar subjects, an interest in physiognomy attracted Toulouse-Lautrec to the popular entertainers of the *café-concerts*. The range and expressive potential of their facial features, particularly when seen in the glare and color of footlights or tinted spots, offered Toulouse-Lautrec an unending outlet for his art of discovering character in outward appearance [29]. The brightness of footlights in Toulouse-Lautrec's oil-on-cardboard portrayal of Irish singer *May Belfort* (active 1890s) [30] heightened the irony of a worldly music-hall entertainer appearing as an innocent little girl. Depicted in pastel colors and dressed like an English moppet with long ringlets and a ruffled bonnet, she stood absolutely stiff onstage, usually clutching a black cat (not seen in this depiction) and singing, "I've got a little cat and I'm very fond of that."

The directness with which Toulouse-Lautrec portrayed celebrities like May Belfort or Yvette Guilbert produced frank, sometimes unflattering, images which on occasion aroused the vanity of the subject and the ire of the critics. One such incident involved a drawing

31 Betty Rubinstein, *Isadora Returns*, 1960.

(dated 1894; Figure 9) that Toulouse-Lautrec did of Guilbert;[15] it may have been a study for a poster commission which eventually went to the artist Théophile Alexandre Steinlen. Guilbert, who preferred Steinlen's more flattering image for *Ambassadeurs: Yvette Guilbert Tous les Soirs*, objected to Toulouse-Lautrec's portrayal and sent him a note, dated July 1894, which read: "For the love of heaven, don't make me so appallingly ugly! Just a little less so! So many people who saw it here shrieked with horror at the sight of your coloured sketch."[16]

The sometimes-exaggerated realism of Toulouse-Lautrec's celebrity portraits is matched by the theatrical images of the American John Sloan (1871-1951), a leading member of a group called The Eight. Like many French artists working in the final quarter of the nineteenth century, The Eight painted modern urban scenes. Working primarily in New York during the early decades of the twentieth century, these artists earned the nickname The Ashcan School by depicting all aspects, even the most mundane, of working-class and middle-class life.

Sloan was one of the four Ashcan painters who began their careers as newspaper illustrators. Attending popular theater and dance performances, he observed many theatrical personalities onstage with a reporter's concern for accuracy and detail and the discerning eye of a critic. One of his favorite subjects was the famous and controversial pioneer of modern dance, Isadora Duncan (1878-1927), of whom he did numerous paintings, drawings, and monotypes. The etching of 1915 exhibited here

Figure 9. Henri de Toulouse-Lautrec, French, 1864-1901. *Yvette Guilbert*. Black crayon, 53¼ × 28¾ inches (135.3 × 73 cm.), ca. 1894. The Cleveland Museum of Art, Leonard C. Hanna Jr. Collection. 50.455.

[32] was carefully worked out in twenty-nine states which were printed in different colors of ink at various stages of development.[17] The attention paid to this print (with all the reworkings) indicates not only a meticulous working method but also the great admiration Sloan had for Isadora Duncan, whose highly expressive movement and choice of loosely falling tunic as opposed to traditional tights reflected her concern with the revival of classical Greek style and form in dance. Despite Sloan's frank appraisal of Duncan's physical appearance—"She was quite heavy, but still beautiful"—the detailed comments in his diaries and other texts confirm his great interest in her as a person and as a dancer: "When this great American and international high priestess of the dance returned from France at the outbreak of World War I, for her first appearance in two years after the tragic death of her children, she lacked slenderness, but was still, in my opinion, the greatest dancer on earth."[18]

Yet, always the objective observer of human life and activity, Sloan did not allow his praise for Duncan, a dancer who "would bring tears to my eyes," to color his portrayal of her onstage. He presented her honestly, exactly as he viewed her—or as we would—from his seat in the audience.

1. From Elizabethan times on, engravings, woodcuts, and sketches were commonly made to document a stage production. The various settings used during the course of a play or ballet were preserved as printed images. Likewise, the performers were portrayed in prints costumed and posed for the roles they played. In many cases these prints provide the only visual record of a memorable production and performance, and consequently, they now illustrate the literature on theater history. For a compilation of many such images see George Altman et al., *Theater Pictorial* (Berkeley and Los Angeles: University

32 John Sloan, *Isadora Duncan*, 1915.

of California Press, 1953), or Bamber Gascoigne, *World Theatre: An Illustrated History* (Toronto: Little, Brown and Company, 1968).

2. Quoted in Phyllis Hartnoll, ed., *The Oxford Companion to the Theatre*, 3rd ed. (London: Oxford University Press, 1967), p. 479.

3. Quoted in Arnold Rood, *Edward Gordon Craig: Artist of the Theatre 1872-1966*, exh. cat. (New York: New York Public Library, 1967), p. 26.

4. Ibid.

5. After failing to sell a painting because the prospective client found his signature distracting, Whistler signed his initials "JMW" in a decorative configuration resembling a butterfly. At times, the monogram was indistinguishable either as initials or as a butterfly, which is the case in this drawing. The initials can barely be seen just to the left of the dancer's skirt.

6. Toulouse-Lautrec was among the other artists who were fascinated by Loie Fuller; see Richard Thomson, *Toulouse-Lautrec* (London: Oresko Books, 1977), p. 67, pl. 41. The flowing dress in Whistler's drawing brings to mind Isadora Duncan's revealing costumes. Duncan was a member of Loie Fuller's touring company in the late 1890s before making a solo tour of Munich, Berlin, Vienna, and Budapest. Her appearances with Fuller's company in Paris, however, were strictly for private audiences. Unless Whistler was invited to one of these exclusive performances, it is unlikely that he would have seen her and singled her out, as his death in 1903 preceded her triumphant return to Western Europe.

7. Getscher, *The Stamp of Whistler*, exh. cat. (Oberlin, Ohio: Allen Memorial Art Museum, 1977); on page 13 he quotes Whistler citing "The Red Rag," 1878, reprinted in *The Gentle Art of Making Enemies* (New York: G. P. Putnam 1953), p. 126.

8. Lillian Browse, *Degas Dancers* (London: Faber and Faber, 1949), p. 53. Theodore Reff also discusses the parallel Degas most likely drew between the dancers and his own "strenuous efforts" in "Edgar Degas and the Dance," *Arts Magazine*, 53 (November 1978), 147.

9. Lillian Browse, in *Degas Dancers*, names three definite productions known to be depicted by Degas: (1) *Semiramis*, 1860, a four-act opera by Mery, and a ballet with music by Carafa based on Rossini's opera *Semiramide*, 1825; (2) Saint-Léon's ballet of 1866, *La Source*; (3) the *Ballet of the Nuns* in Meyerbeer's opera *Robert le Diable*, 1871, which was revived numerous times after its premiere in 1831. According to Browse three other ballets are identifiable in Degas's work (p. 56). She also remarks, on p. 60, "As far as is known he has inscribed the names of only four different dancers on his drawings and in three cases they are dancers of no importance who would

probably never have been heard of but through their connection with him."

10. Theodore Reff, in "Edgar Degas and the Dance," *Arts Magazine* 53 (November 1978), 149, attributes this insistence on depicting *tutus* to the artist's appreciation of "time-honored" customs and the fact that for Degas, classical ballet "evoked the truly classical art of ancient Greece." Reff cites Browse (p. 54; see note 8 above) in noting the artistic license taken by Degas in the depiction of rehearsal clothes as well. To the usual attire of long white *tutus* and flesh-colored tights he added bright, colorful sashes and black velvet chokers.

11. Browse, *Degas Dancers*, p. 46, offers a list of the great names in ballet who had retired by mid-century.

12. Ibid., p. 63.

13. Richard Thomson, *Toulouse-Lautrec*, p. 14.

14. *Portraits of the American Stage*, exh. cat. (Washington, D.C.: Smithsonian Institution Press for the National Portrait Gallery, 1971), pp. 82-83. The description of Loie Fuller's stage effects points up her serious interest in light. She befriended Pierre and Marie Curie and learned much from their remarkable work. Experimental by nature, she constantly elaborated her productions to such a complex level that for some of them—for example, Fire Dance—she eventually required the services of a dozen or more electricians and numerous stagehands. Her innovations in lighting and stagecraft by far surpassed her contribution, if any, to choreography—a summation which would have pleased her. She declared herself the "only person who is known as a dancer but who has a personal preference for science."

15. A repair made in this drawing before it was acquired by the Museum has recently become visible.

16. Quoted in Thomson, *Toulouse-Lautrec*, p. 82, pl. 53.

17. Peter Morse, *John Sloan's Prints: A Catalogue Raisonné of the Etchings, Lithographs, and Posters* (New Haven and London: Yale University Press, 1969), no. 172, pp. 195ff.

18. Various sources with selected comments by Sloan about Isadora Duncan are quoted from or referred to in Morse, *John Sloan's Prints*, p. 176.

The Audience

Attending a stage production of any sort can be considered a type of theater in and of itself. We costume and "prop" ourselves with whatever we think would be appropriate, and sometimes we make do with whatever is available. We prepare ourselves for the role we will play as spectators: either we consciously and methodically develop an audience character similar to a reporter, critic, or artist; or we wait for the action to begin, at which time we can improvise our parts as occasional theatergoers or seasonal regulars. We are an untrained amateur cast who, like the professionals, create an audience scene together yet act with individual style and personal approach.

Enter the artist, costumed in spectator clothes with program and pencil as props, who takes a seat. In character, as audience member, he watches the production and partakes in the overall theatrical experience. But in a special role as an artist-observer within an audience of spectators, he convincingly interprets his part in visual terms by drawing and sketching not only the action on stage but also the full range of audience persona surrounding him.

Occasionally the artist will discover his drama in the audience itself. The American Edward Hopper (1882-1967) in almost all his theater scenes turned his attention to the audience, presenting, as in *Two on the Aisle* (Figure 10), just one or a few people waiting for the play to begin or to resume. Like the director, an artist may spotlight a dramatic or comic

Figure 10. Edward Hopper, American, 1882-1967. *Two on the Aisle*. Oil on canvas, 40⅛ × 48¼ inches (102 × 122.5 cm.), 1927. The Toledo Museum of Art, Gift of Edward Drummond Libbey. 35.49.

interaction—but among members of the audience rather than among the players. Making meaningful selections of lighting, props, gesture, and expression in order to create the appropriate mood, he "blocks out" the audience scene before, between, during, and after the production onstage.

33 Gerard Cochet, *Theatre.*

In the lithograph entitled *Theatre* [33] French painter-illustrator-etcher Gerard Paul Cochet (1888-1969) skillfully uses dark and light tones to evoke the heightened dramatic effects of theater. He emphasizes three young ladies in the audience by placing them in a neutral background with few details. The women are completely absorbed in the show and seem to be unconsciously huddled together. The figure on the right raises her left hand to her head and absentmindedly adjusts her hat or perhaps straightens a loose strand of hair. The dark, indistinct forms of the women's bodies would merge together completely were they not clarified with highlighted areas which reveal faces, a portion of the raised hand on the right, a coat worn by the central figure, and the program (suggested by a blank, white area of paper). The woman on the right rests her arm on a ledge next to her which runs obliquely up from the central foreground toward the right edge of the image. Jutting in from the right corner and perpendicular to the ledge on which they, too, rest are additional programs (barely delineated with a few quick lines of Cochet's lithographic crayon). While we view the women straight on, almost full-faced, the implied line of their gaze, which is averted from us as they intently watch the stage, follows the angle of the ledge.

The sketchy quality and oblique angle of the overall image as well as the partial view of programs and seats all contribute to a sense of immediacy. Furthermore, Cochet's fast lines and energetic shading capture the feeling of a performance in progress and the urgency of quick costume and set changes between scenes, or of warning bells recalling the audience after intermission. Because lithography, more so than any other printmaking medium, can transmit the spontaneous, expressive qualities of drawing, Cochet undoubtedly found it well-suited to the realities of stage production and audience experience.

A comprehensive view of theatrical experience is one that simultaneously presents the action not only onstage but in the audience as well. For example, from a specific seat in the orchestra or balcony Toulouse-Lautrec—and on occasion even the detached Degas—depicted what was quite literally before him. As Charles Stuckey notes, one of Toulouse-Lautrec's favorite themes was "the relationship between sincerity and pretense or reality and theater, and that between observer and observed, actor and spectator."[1] In

Toulouse-Lautrec's work, or in pictures like Georges Seurat's *Café-Concert* [34], Everett Shinn's theatrical scenes [36-40], or Béraud's outdoor *café-concert* [35], the views of the stage (complete with the heads and figures of spectators seen from the rear) point up not only the parallels between the imaginary world onstage and the "real" world before it but also draw a connection between the spectators observing a performance and the spectators who view the artist's conception of that performance.

In *Café-Concert* [34], Seurat makes little distinction between the viewer in his audience and the spectator he depicts in the theater observing the singer onstage. By implication they are the same. With a style and technique which effectively eliminates the use of line and nonessential detail, and by placing his viewer right in the middle of the crowd, Seurat provides an amazingly naturalistic ambience despite the geometric abstraction characteristic of his forms and figures. The sense of being part of a full audience is heightened both by the compact composition and a view of the stage which is obstructed by strategically placed derby hats. The partial view of the man closest to us fills the right side of the image, giving us a familiar, if somewhat unpleasant, impression of having our way out of the crowd blocked. In the lower portion of the image, velvety, thick dark tones of the greasy conté crayon are molded into simple geometric shapes representing figures in the audience. These are contrasted with three touches of white crayon (for footlights) and with the light areas in the upper portion of the image that represent the brightly lit stage area. The slim figure of

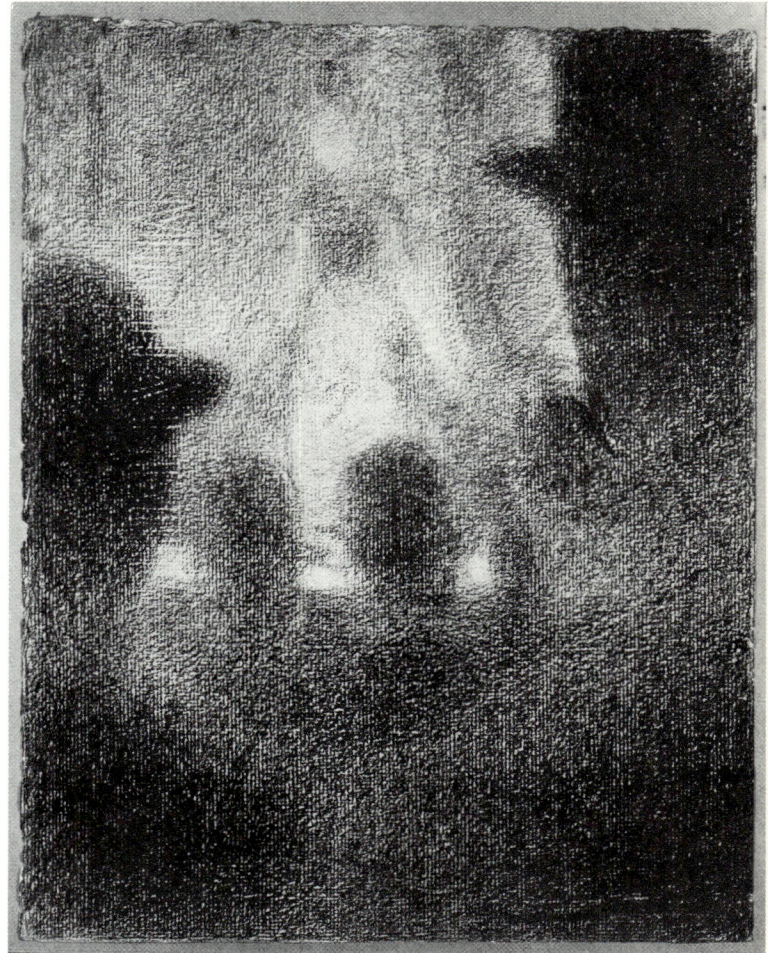

34 Georges Seurat, *Café-Concert*, ca. 1887.

the female singer is barely decipherable, although the gaiety of her presence, indeed the overall atmosphere of the cabaret scene, is strongly felt.

Georges Seurat (1859-1891), whose mature career spanned little more than a decade before his untimely death at the age of thirty-two, completed some 500 drawings, only seventy-five of which were actually studies for paintings.[2] His studious approach to aesthetics and technique resulted in a highly individualized, rigid (though effective) approach to the interpretation of human experience in visual terms. Most of the problem-solving, the experimentation, and the testing of his theories was accomplished in his drawings, for Seurat completed only seven major paintings. He emphasized contrasts—of light and dark; of directional, not actual, lines; of complementary colors in his paintings—and preferred the use of simple geometric shapes or continuous masses. Scanning first the peasant, then urban, and finally the night life of his time, Seurat managed to extract the monumental and universal qualities of human experience from the specifics of subject matter. Whereas the sparse details of Cochet's tonal lithograph pinpoint a moment in time and suggest immediacy, Seurat's generalized forms in *Café-Concert* evoke reality frozen in time; the figures remain both observing and observed in a universal moment.

Seurat's concert group—consisting of four or five drawings done around 1887—examined the specific problem of how "to represent an audience in shadow listening to a singer on a strongly lighted stage, indoors."[3] If Seurat was more the serious, detached theoretician whose interest in theater scenes probably arose from the desire to solve a self–appointed problem, then the American Everett Shinn (1876-1953) was the playful illustrator whose newspaper background and lively

36   Everett Shinn, *Irving Theatre*, 1924.

personality gave his theater scenes a special flair. His interest in theater was a long–standing and fully involved one. He, too, grappled with a visual problem— the rendering of artificial and heightened stage lighting. But Shinn's fast sketchy style comes nowhere near the perceptive study evident in just one of Seurat's concert drawings.

Consider, however, that Everett Shinn was trained as a newspaper artist, an experience from which he undoubtedly developed a sharp eye, quick hand, and narrative skills. Aided by a phenomenal memory, Shinn painted facilely, a talent which, as suggested by Ira Glackens, William Glackens's son, may have worked against him in the end: Shinn's "inability to concentrate what came so easily" meant that he never fully worked out his ideas and visions. "His theatrical canvases, with their great mastery of artificial light . . . , after one has been sufficiently stunned by their technical brilliance, turn out to be curiously shallow."[4]

Shinn was restless in the audience and, like the newspaper reporter, studied the scene just long enough to get the facts and cover the story. His emphasis on narrative and his interest in depicting the scenarios of daily life in New York City at the turn of the century reflect the concerns he shared with the group of artists called The Eight. (Three others among The Eight had been newspaper artists like Shinn—William J. Glackens, George Luks, and John Sloan.) This group's honest, straightforward coverage of life in the streets of modern urban society showed not only an affinity for the realism of the late nineteenth–century American Thomas Eakins but also a similarity to the French Naturalists, such as Raffaelli, Degas, or Toulouse–Lautrec, and many others whose subject matter covered the broad spectrum of human activity.

Shinn's music–hall scenes [37-39] are lively impressions of popular evening entertainment in New York. The same immediate and quickly sketched qualities also characterize the painting by Jean Béraud (1849-1935) of a

37 Everett Shinn, *Music Hall Scene*, ca. 1948.

38 Everett Shinn, *Music Hall Scene*, ca. 1948.

39 Everett Shinn, *Little Theater*, 1950.

40 Everett Shinn, *Dancer in White*, 1910.

Parisian outdoor night spot with entertainers *Valmy and Lea* [35]. In all these images the artist's viewpoint and, by implication, ours, is from the audience, although Béraud might have been a casual passerby who paused for a moment from a street promenade to observe the high–kicking, arm–raising song and dance act onstage. In all these scenes the inclusion of audience and orchestra members seen from the rear or in profile reflect the artist's desire to present in a natural manner the overall scene as well as to communicate the experience of being there.

Certain deliberate effects in these sketches and the two other works by Shinn, *Irving Theater* [36] and *Dancer in White* [40], serve as more than visual connectors. For example, the horizontal row of street lights hovering over the audience in the right half of Béraud's outdoor scene [35] not only parallels the line of hats merged together below but also alludes to the bawdy nature of the entertainment, for the lights seem to disappear into the female dancer's petticoats under a leg kicked high in a can–can step, the popular dance rage at the time known as *le chahut*. In the same picture a well–dressed man in tophat stands in the right foreground and calls to someone "offstage" or perhaps to the attendant in the left corner holding a sign announcing the next act. Again, the street lights do more than merely illuminate: by following the path of the spoken message, they call attention to the foreground action and add a touch of intrigue.

Another notable element in Béraud's picture is present also in Shinn's works [39, 40]: the protruding scroll end of the double bass. A familiar motif that recalls the ballet scenes of Degas in the 1880s, the bass scroll asserted the presence of the unseen orchestra, offered a visual link between the audience and the performer onstage, and contributed a certain authen-

ticity to any music– or dance–hall scene. As both Lillian Browse and Theodore Reff point out in their respective studies of Degas's dancers, the scroll was a visual element Degas used suggestively in relationship to the dancer's position onstage, and, borrowed from Degas, the scroll motif was later used more explicitly by Toulouse–Lautrec in his famous poster of Jane Avril at the Jardin de Paris.[5]

The double–bass scroll in Shinn's *Dancer in White* [40], however, carries a different meaning: it appears primarily as a descriptive feature. Compositionally it serves as a vertical counterpart on the right to the standing woman seen along the left edge, and the shape of the scroll end is echoed visually by the spiral of the short railing just above it on stage.

As in Béraud's outdoor concert, the action and drama in Shinn's painting appear as much in the audience as onstage. While Shinn does seem to linger over the build–up of flowing white paint in the dancer's dress, he takes some of the attention away from the performer by allowing a darkly dressed, elegant woman in the foreground to stand up, turn around, and look back into the audience. The implied diagonal line of her raised and gloved hands is continued into the lines of the dancer's dress, through the lean of the dancer's upper body and the position of her arms. The final element of audience–viewer interaction, however, occurs in the intent glance of a man seated to the right of the standing woman. Barely visible in the space between the heads of two ladies wearing plumed hats, the man also turns around and peers out, but not at some unseen person in the audience. Instead, he seems to be looking at us, the viewers, which not only establishes our position in the audience and points up the double meaning of our role as observers but also alludes to the artist's role as interpolator. This detail of

Figure 11. Photograph: *Everett Shinn*. Ca. 1920. Everett Shinn Collection, Delaware Art Museum, Wilmington, Delaware.

role of performers or spectators, the experience of being in the audience can have a profound effect on the lifestyle and work of an artist. In Edward Hopper's case, for example, "frequent attendance at plays and movies [with his wife Jo, who was both a fellow painter and former actress] had two direct effects on his paintings: his choice of theaters as subject matter and the development of compositions that were often influenced by set design, stage lighting, and cinematic devices such as cropping and unusual angles of vision."[6] A theatrical type of lighting, with strong light and dark contrasts, plus a heightened sense of moment infuse many of the paintings by Hopper, whether of a theatrical subject or not. As Gail Levin points out, his renowned view of a typical deserted street in *Early Sunday Morning* (Figure 12) may actually have been inspired by Jo Mielziner's set (Figure 13) for *Street Scene*, a play by Elmer Rice.[7] The Hoppers attended the production at the Playhouse Theater in New York in January 1929, viewing the play and its set from the second balcony. Not only are the type of buildings and general layout similar in Mielziner's set and Hopper's painting, but the same high vantage point from which Hopper viewed the set is repeated in *Early Sunday Morning*, here with the implication that the viewer looks at buildings across the street from a second–floor room.

the man's face looking back in our direction could be a self–portrait (Figure 11), or at least, a reference to the artist himself who sits in the theater, views both the players on stage and members of the audience, and then, with selected visual devices—spectators facing away from the stage or a music stand partially included in a lower corner—pulls the viewer into the scene and summarizes the connections among all.

Aside from providing visual stimulus for the artist and bringing about his personal identification with the

Figure 12. Edward Hopper. *Early Sunday Morning*. Oil on canvas, 35 × 60 inches (88.9 × 152.4 cm.), 1930. Collection of the Whitney Musuem of American Art. (Photograph by Geoffrey Clements)

Figure 13. Set for *Street Scene* by Elmer Rice at the Playhouse Theater, 1929. The exterior of an apartment house in a mean quarter of New York, end of Act II; set design by Jo Mielziner. White Photo, Theater and Music Collection, Museum of the City of New York.

For Shinn, the theater subjects he painted and sketched offered merely one outlet for a lifelong interest in the stage and performance, which had been activated by a typical childhood fascination for circuses and parades. His interest in the theater found its first expression in the posters that he made for his brother, Warren, who ran the dances at the Opera House in their hometown of Woodstown, New Jersey.[8]

Later, the first opportunity to participate directly in theater came, ironically, out of his association with The Pennsylvania Academy of Fine Arts, where he enrolled to study painting in 1893. The group of students who met regularly at Robert Henri's studio (Henri was teaching at the Academy then) produced a takeoff on George

Figure 14. Photograph: *Party at the Shinns, 112 Waverly Place*. Ca. 1912. John Sloan Collection, Delaware Art Museum, Wilmington, Delaware.

DuMaurier's *Trilby* which they called *Twillbee*.[9] Shinn made his acting debut in this farce as the expatriate painter James McNails Whiskers.[10] His active role in the stage world also included designing wall panels and murals to decorate David Belasco's Stuyvesant Theater, which opened in New York in 1907.

But the total integration of art and theater in Everett Shinn's life occurred around the year 1912, when he produced a group of dramatic pieces at his studio on Waverly Place in New York. He had built a small, yet complete, theater with a proscenium stage and a house capacity of fifty-five.[11] Shinn performed with The Waverly Street Players, an amateur group he formed of fellow artists and various other friends, in plays which were also written, directed, and designed by him.[12] Even the parties at the Shinn studio residence reflected his theatrical leanings and lively personality. Friends often arrived in costume carrying musical instruments and they were not bashful about posing in the street for photographs (Figure 14). In flavor, these gatherings, enlivened as they were by the creative merrymaking of Shinn's artist and writer friends, were not unlike the annual "bal-masque" of Cleveland's Kokoon Arts Club, announced each year by a poster/invitation [21] designed by one of the artist members. Composed of Cleveland area artists, the Kokoon Arts Club thrived in the twenties and, like Shinn's Players, seems to have been essentially a social organization dedicated to self-entertainment.[13]

Like Edward Gordon Craig, Shinn found art and acting inextricably linked through a common denominator: the interpretation of human experience. But, whereas Craig came to art trained as an actor and remained essentially a theater person, Shinn was first the artist-reporter whose desire to be in the spotlight was balanced by and, perhaps in the end, dominated by the need to watch and record the action unobserved. Most of Shinn's theatrical subjects reflect not his own experiences onstage, but rather offer overall views of performances in progress, in which the artist more closely identifies with the audience than with the performers.[14]

As an artist-designer-writer-producer, like the Futurist Enrico Prampolini, Shinn's involvement in the stage world was a multi-faceted one and resulted in a theater that was completely his own. His pursuit of stage production, however, was not motivated by theoretical, aesthetic, or social issues as it was for Prampolini and most of the other visual artists who have created theater, including contemporary performance artists. Taking advantage of the transient nature of theater productions and making use of modern technology, Futurists, Constructivists, and Bauhaus artists saw the stage as a testing ground to work out their respective concepts of art.

Shinn, however, experienced the theater—whether onstage performing or offstage observing—as a playground. The stage, at best, satisfied the needs of a dramatic yet playful personality and had less effect on his paintings than did his detached observations. Even as artist-observer, the lighting effects he captured and the numerous audience views he presented reflect the interests and experience of a stagestruck spectator, not the concerns of a painter seeking visual solutions.

The stage scenes of Shinn, Béraud, Seurat, and the other artist-spectators place equal if not greater emphasis on the views of or from the audience. The fact that the performers onstage share the spotlight with members of the audience affirms a universal concept of theater as a microcosm of the real world. This concept is the thread that runs through the stage designs and theories of the artist-participants, and it is the one we bring with us when we enter the theater. If all the world's a stage, as Shakespeare tells us, then surely it must follow that the stage holds all the world.

1. Charles F. Stuckey, *Toulouse-Lautrec: Paintings*, exh. cat. (Chicago: The Art Institute of Chicago, 1980), p. 139.
2. Robert Herbert, "Seurat's Drawings," in *Seurat: Paintings and Drawings*, edited by Daniel Catton Rich (Chicago: The Art Institute of Chicago, 1958), p. 22.
3. Germain Seligman, *The Drawings of Georges Seurat* (New York: Curt Valentin, 1947), p. 24.
4. From Ira Glackens's introductory remarks in Edith DeShazo, *Everett Shinn, 1876-1953: A Figure in His Time* (New York: Clarkson N. Potter, 1974), p. xvi.
5. Lillian Browse, *Degas Dancers* (London: Faber and Faber, 1949), p. 42, and Theodore Reff, "Edgar Degas and the Dance," *Arts Magazine* 53 (November 1978), 149. Charles Stuckey (see note 1 above),

on page 207, offers a candid description of this motif in the Jane Avril image: "In this poster, the dancer lifts her black-stockinged leg to reveal a flounce of petticoats, as if to tantalize the orchestra's rather grotesque bass viol player, whose instrument's neck erectly salutes her flirtation."
6. Gail Levin, *Edward Hopper: The Art and the Artist*, exh. cat. (New York: W. W. Norton and Company for The Whitney Museum of American Art, 1980), p. 53.
7. Ibid., pp. 57-58.
8. Edith DeShazo, *Everett Shinn*, p. 71.
9. Originally a novel by George DuMaurier (1834-1896), who was an English artist, *Trilby* was dramatized in 1895 with great success; Phyllis Hartnoll, ed., *The Oxford Companion to the Theatre*, 3rd ed. (London: Oxford University Press, 1967), p. 259.
10. Bennard Perlman, *The Immortal Eight* (New York: Exposition Press, 1962), p. 68.
11. Edith DeShazo, *Everett Shinn*, p. 71.
12. Shinn continued to write short plays and novellas throughout his life. The early plays performed by The Waverly Street Players were mostly parody melodramas with such titles as *Ethel Clayton or Wronged from the Start* and *Lucy Moore or the Prune Hater's Daughter*. While they revealed his farcical humor and highly dramatic personal style, as Ira Glackens (whose mother and artist father William appeared in these early plays) points out: "The text of his plays reads as if dashed off in an hour, without revision. His wonderful ideas are not worked out, and many a fine effect is half-realized." Glackens softens the nature of his criticism however in recognizing that Shinn's melodramas were done to "please no one but himself, his actors, and his audience, and all this he did with abundant success," in Edith DeShazo, *Everett Shinn*, p. xvi. Shinn's plays never won critical acclaim (a review of *Prune Hater's Daughter* appeared in *The New York Times* on March 21, 1912, with the headline "Artists as Actors Give Prune Drama"), but DeShazo claims some "were eventually bought and incorporated into vaudeville acts," p. 80.
13. Little is known about the Kokoon Arts Club or its members. Viktor Schreckengost, an artist teaching at the Cleveland Institute of Art, whose own work for theater included the first stage design ever to make the cover of *Theatre Arts Monthly* (December 1941), reminisced about the club to the author in a phone conversation, December 1980. He recalled that the club was social in nature and was distinguished from the more serious professional groups of artists meeting formally at the time.
14. There were a few images created from the performer's point of view, looking out into the audience: for example, *Curtain Call* (in Ira and Nancy Glackens's collection reproduced in Edith DeShazo, *Everett Shinn*, pp. 46-47); a drawing in red chalk, *The Magician* (St. Louis Museum of Art, see DeShazo, p. 49); and *Dancer on Stage* (in DeShazo, pp. 160-61).

Catalog

1 Yale University drama students under the direction of Dr. Elemer Nagy, American, contemporary. *Model of a Naturalist Setting Designed by Donald Oenslager for a Scene from "Of Mice and Men" by John Steinbeck.* Mixed media, 32⅛ inches (81.6 cm.). Theater Arts Area, Cleveland State University, Cleveland, Ohio.

2 Léon Bakst, Russian, 1866-1924. *Design for a Stage Set.* Pencil, 13³⁄₁₆ × 6⅝ inches (33.5 × 16.8 cm.), 1915. The Cleveland Museum of Art, Dudley P. Allen Fund. 79.92

3 Natalia Gontcharova, Russian, 1881-1962. *Two-Piece Squid Costume for the Ballet "Sadko."* Silk and other textiles; dress length 40 inches (101.6 cm.); headdress height 21 inches (53.3 cm.); ca. 1916. Allen Memorial Art Museum, Oberlin College, Oberlin, Ohio; Purchase, Charles F. Olney Fund. 68.44

4 Natalia Gontcharova. *Fish Headdress for the Ballet "Sadko."* Silk, sequins, cotton-backing, 15 × 34½ inches (38.1 × 87.6 cm.), ca. 1916. Allen Memorial Art Museum, Oberlin College, Oberlin, Ohio; Helen Ward Memorial Costume Collection Fund. 69.38

5 Simon Lissim, American (born Russia), 1900-. *The Yellow Sultan.* Gouache on paper, 39⅜ × 28 inches (100 × 71.1 cm.), 1939. Columbus Museum of Art, Columbus, Ohio; Howald Fund Purchase.

6 Eugene Berman, American (born Russia), 1899-1972. *Costume Study.* Ink on cardboard, 8¾ × 7⅝ inches (22.2 × 19.3 cm.), 1945. Allen Memorial Art Museum, Oberlin College, Oberlin, Ohio; Gift of Monroe Wheeler and Mauricio Aguilar. 49.23

7 Yale University drama students under the direction of Dr. Elemer Nagy. *Model of an Abstract Setting Designed by Adolphe Appia for "Iphigenia in Aulis."* Mixed media, 32⅛ inches (81.6 cm.). Theater Arts Area, Cleveland State University, Cleveland, Ohio.

8 Yale University drama students under the direction of Dr. Elemer Nagy. *Model of an Abstract Setting Designed by Edward Gordon Craig.* Mixed media, 32⅛ inches (81.6 cm.). Theater Arts Area, Cleveland State University, Cleveland, Ohio.

9 Edward Gordon Craig, British, 1872-1966. *Design for a Stage Scene.* Woodcut, 3¼ × 2¹⁄₁₆ inches (8.2 × 5.3 cm.); block executed 1900, printed 1923. The Cleveland Museum of Art, Gift of The Print Club of Cleveland. 24.338

10 Edward Gordon Craig. *Design for a Stage Scene.* Woodcut, 2¼ × 4⅝ inches (5.7 × 11.8 cm.); block executed 1900, printed 1923. The Cleveland Museum of Art, Gift of The Print Club of Cleveland. 24.336

11 Yale University drama students under the direction of Dr. Elemer Nagy. *Model of a Constructivist Setting Designed by Georgii Yakulov for "Girofle-Girofla" by Offenbach.* Mixed media, 32⅛ inches (81.6 cm.). Theater Arts Area, Cleveland State University, Cleveland, Ohio.

12 Edward Gordon Craig. *A Comic Mask.* Woodcut, 2⅞ × 3¼ inches (7.3 × 8.2 cm.); block executed 1910, printed 1923. The Cleveland Museum of Art, Gift of The Print Club of Cleveland. 24.339

13 Edward Gordon Craig. *Sketch for Headgear for "Hamlet."* Pencil on cloth, 8 × 5 inches (20.3 × 12.7 cm.), 1912. Special Collections Department, Northwestern University Library, Evanston, Illinois.

14 George Grosz, American (born Germany), 1893-1959. *Student: Design for Goll's "Methusalem."* Water color on paper, 20½ × 14½ inches (52 × 36.8 cm.), 1922. Contemporary Collection of The Cleveland Museum of Art. 66.50

15 Jules Chéret, French, 1836-1932. *Viviane.* Color lithograph, 30⅞ × 22⅛ inches (78.4 × 56.2 cm.), 1886. The Cleveland Museum of Art, The Harold T. Clark Educational Extension Fund. 72.1126

16 Jules Chéret. *Olympia.* Color lithograph, 49 x 39½ inches (124.5 × 100.3 cm.), 1892. Anonymous Loan.

17 Jules Chéret. *Folies Bergère, Fleur de Lotus.* Color lithograph, 48¼ × 34¼ inches (122.6 × 87 cm.), 1893. Allen Memorial Art Museum, Oberlin College, Oberlin, Ohio; Purchase, Show Fund. 58.186

18 Alphonse Maria Mucha, Czechoslovakian, 1860-1939. *La Samaritaine.* Color lithograph, 67 × 21⁹⁄₁₆ inches (170 × 54.7 cm.), 1897. The Cleveland Museum of Art, L. E. Holden Fund. 68.215

19 Alphonse Maria Mucha. *Lorenzaccio.* Color lithograph, 15 × 6 inches (38.1 × 15.2 cm.), 1899. The Cleveland Museum of Art, The Harold T. Clark Educational Extension Fund. 73.1018

20 Emanuel-Joseph-Raphael Orazi, Italian (French School), 1860-1934. *Palais de la Danse.* Color lithograph, 61 × 23 inches (154.9 × 58.4 cm.). Joseph M. Erdelac Collection, Cleveland, Ohio.

21 Joseph W. Jicha, American (Cleveland School), 1901-1960. *Kokoon Arts Club, Bal des Arts—Poster/Invitation.* Color lithograph, 40 × 26¼ inches (101.6 × 66.7 cm.), 1928. The Western Reserve Historical Society, Cleveland, Ohio.

22 Edward Gordon Craig. *Henry Irving as "Badger."* Woodcut, 4¼ × 3¼ inches (10.8 × 8.3 cm.); block executed 1900, printed 1924. The Cleveland Museum of Art, Gift of The Print Club of Cleveland. 24.340

23 William Nicholson, English, 1872-1949. *Sarah Bernhardt.* Woodcut, 15³⁄₁₆ × 14⅛ inches (38.5 × 35.8 cm.), 1964 (second edition). Allen Memorial Art Museum, Oberlin College, Oberlin, Ohio; C. F. Olney Fund. 68.45 (First edition, in color, published in 1899 by Heinemann, London; second edition published by Lord's Gallery, London.)

24 James Abbott McNeill Whistler, American, 1834-1903. *The Dancer, No. 1 (Connie Gilchrist).* Pen and ink, 4⁵⁄₁₆ × 5⅞ inches (10.9 × 14.9 cm.). The Cleveland Museum of Art, Gift of Mr. and Mrs. Ralph King. 24.90

25 Hilaire Germain Edgar Degas, French, 1834-1917. *Ballet Girls.* Pastel, 21¾ × 16³⁄₁₆ inches (55.2 × 41.1 cm.). The Cleveland Museum of Art, Gift of Mr. and Mrs. J. H. Wade. 16.1043

26 Hilaire Germain Edgar Degas. *Ballet Dancer.* Charcoal (counterproof), 16¾ × 12⅞ inches (42.5 × 32.7 cm.). The Cleveland Museum of Art, Gift of Ralph King. 24.329

27 Henri de Toulouse-Lautrec, French, 1864-1901. *Miss Loie Fuller.* Lithograph printed in colors, 10⅛ × 15 inches (25.7 × 38.1 cm.), 1893. The Cleveland Museum of Art, Gift of Ralph King. 25.1202

28 Henri de Toulouse-Lautrec. *Yvette Guilbert* (English Series). Lithograph, 20 × 15¼ inches (50.5 × 39 cm.), 1898. The Cleveland Museum of Art, Mr. and Mrs. Charles G. Prasse Collection. 56.616 (This is the frontispiece of a complete bound set of ten lithographs.)

29 Henri de Toulouse-Lautrec. *Yvette Guilbert: On Stage* (No. 1 in English Series). Lithograph, 12¾ × 10½ inches (32.3 × 26.5 cm.), 1898. The Cleveland Museum of Art, Mr. and Mrs. Lewis B. Williams Collection. 42.1061

30 Henri de Toulouse-Lautrec. *May Belfort.* Oil on cardboard, 24¾ × 19 inches (62.9 × 48.3 cm.), 1895. The Cleveland Museum of Art, Purchase, Leonard C. Hanna Jr. Bequest. 58.54

31 Betty Rubinstein, American, contemporary. *Isadora Returns.* Ink on paper, 19½ × 13½ inches (49.5 × 34.3 cm.), 1960. The Butler Institute of American Art, Youngstown, Ohio (Gift of Louis Held).

32 John Sloan, American, 1871-1951. *Isadora Duncan.* Etching, 8¹⁵⁄₁₆ × 7⅜ inches (22.7 × 18.7 cm.), 1915. The Cleveland Museum of Art, Gift of Mrs. Malcolm L. McBride. 59.301

33 Gerard Cochet, French, 1888-1969. *Theatre.* Lithograph, 7⅛ × 10⅛ inches (18 × 25.7 cm.). The Cleveland Museum of Art, Gift of The Print Club of Cleveland. 31.257

34 Georges Seurat, French, 1859-1891. *Café-Concert.* Conté crayon heightened with white, 12⅜ × 9⁵⁄₁₆ inches (30.5-31.5 × 23.8 cm.), ca. 1887. The Cleveland Museum of Art, Purchase, Leonard C. Hanna Jr. Bequest. 58.344

35 Jean Béraud, French, 1849-1935. *Valmy and Lea.* Gouache (?) on paper, 19⅝ × 13½ inches (49.8 × 34.3 cm.). Mrs. Noah L. Butkin Collection, Cleveland, Ohio.

36 Everett Shinn, American, 1876-1953. *Irving Theatre.* Mixed media, 17 × 18½ inches (43.2 × 47 cm.), 1924. The Cleveland Museum of Art, Gift of Mr. and Mrs. Noah L. Butkin. 71.185

37 Everett Shinn. *Music Hall Scene.* Water color with pencil indications, 4¹⁵⁄₁₆ × 3 inches (12.5 × 7.6 cm.), ca. 1948. The Cleveland Museum of Art, Gift of The Print Club of Cleveland. 56.303

38 Everett Shinn. *Music Hall Scene.* Water color with pencil indications, 4¹⁵⁄₁₆ × 2¹⁵⁄₁₆ inches (12.5 × 7.5 cm.), ca. 1948. The Cleveland Museum of Art, Gift of The Print Club of Cleveland. 56.304

39 Everett Shinn. *Little Theater.* Water color with pencil indications, 7½ x 8¹⁄₁₆ inches (19 × 20.5 cm.), 1950. The Cleveland Museum of Art, Gift of Mr. and Mrs. Ralph L. Wilson. 61.165

40 Everett Shinn. *Dancer in White.* Oil on canvas, 35 × 39 inches (88.9 × 99.1 cm.), 1910 (some reworking in 1952). The Butler Institute of American Art, Youngstown, Ohio.

Bibliography

Altman, George; Freud, Ralph; Macgowen, Kenneth; and Melnitz, William. *Theater Pictorial: A History of World Theater as Recorded in Drawings, Paintings, Engravings, and Photographs.* Berkeley and Los Angeles: University of California Press, 1953.

Alexandrian. *Seurat.* New York: Crown Publishers, 1980.

Amberg, George. *Art in Modern Ballet.* New York: Pantheon Books, 1946.

Amberg, George. *The Theatre of Eugene Berman,* exh. cat. New York: The Museum of Modern Art, 1947.

Anderson, John. *The American Theater.* New York: The Dial Press, 1938.

Annenkov, George P. "Russian Painters and the Rebirth of Theatre Arts," in *Russian Stage and Costume Designs for the Ballet, Opera and Theatre,* exh. cat. Washington, D. C.: International Exhibitions Foundation, 1967, pp. 5-8.

Axsom, Richard Hayden. "Parade: Cubism as Theater." Ph.D. dissertation, University of Michigan, 1974; Ann Arbor, Michigan: University Microfilms, 1979.

Bablet, Denis. *Edward Gordon Craig.* Translated by Daphne Woodward. New York: Theatre Arts Books, 1966.

Barron, Stephanie and Tuchman, Maurice. *The Avant-Garde in Russia, 1910-1930: New Perspectives,* exh. cat. Los Angeles: Los Angeles County Museum of Art, 1980.

Beaumont, Cyril W. *Five Centuries of Ballet Design.* London: The Studio Ltd., n. d.

Bowlt, John E. *Diaghilev and Russian Stage Designers,* exh. cat. Washington, D. C.: International Exhibitions Foundation, 1972.

Bowlt, John E. *Stage Designs and the Russian Avant-Garde, 1911-1929,* exh. cat. Washington, D. C.: International Exhibitions Foundation, 1976.

Browse, Lillian. *William Nicholson.* London: Rupert Hart-Davis, 1956.

Buckle, Richard. *Modern Ballet Design.* New York: The MacMillan Company, 1955.

Cooper, Douglas. *Picasso Theatre.* New York: Harry N. Abrams, 1967.

DeShazo, Edith et al. *Everett Shinn 1876-1953,* exh. cat. Trenton, N. J.: New Jersey State Museum, 1973.

DeShazo, Edith. *Everett Shinn 1876-1953: A Figure in His Time.* New York: Clarkson N. Potter, 1974.

Designs by Inigo Jones for Masques and Plays at Court. Oxford: The University Press, 1924. Introduction and notes by Percy Simpson and C. F. Bell.

Diaghilev/Cunningham, exh. cat. Hempstead, N. Y.: The Emily Lowe Gallery, Hofstra University, 1974.

Dreams in the Theatre: Designs of Simon Lissim, exh. cat. New York: The New York Public Library, 1975. Exhibition at Vincent Astor Gallery, Lincoln Center.

Gascoigne, Bamber. *World Theatre: An Illustrated History.* Boston and Toronto: Little, Brown and Company, 1968.

d'Harnoncourt, Anne. *Futurism and the International Avant-Garde,* exh. cat. Philadelphia: Philadelphia Museum of Art, 1980.

Hartnoll, Phyllis. *The Concise History of Theatre.* New York: Harry N. Abrams, 1968.

Hartnoll, Phyllis, ed., *The Oxford Companion to the Theatre,* 3rd ed. London: Oxford University Press, 1967.

Kardon, Janet. *Artists' Sets and Costumes,* exh. cat. Philadelphia: Philadelphia College of Art, 1977.

Kernodle, George R. *From Art To Theatre: Form and Convention in the Renaissance.* Chicago: University of Chicago Press, 1944.

Kirby, Michael. *Futurist Performance.* New York: E. P. Dutton & Co., 1971.

Kochno, Boris. *Diaghilev and the Ballets Russes.* Translated by Adrienne Foulke. New York: Harper & Row, 1970.

Levin, Gail. *Edward Hopper: The Art and the Artist,* exh. cat. New York: W. W. Norton and Company for The Whitney Museum of American Art, 1980.

Morse, Peter. *John Sloan's Prints: A Catalogue Raisonné of the Etchings, Lithographs, and Posters.* New Haven and London: Yale University Press, 1969.

Mucha, Jiri et al. *Alphonse Mucha Posters and Photographs.* New York: St. Martin's Press, 1971.

Muehlig, Linda D. *Degas and the Dance,* exh. cat. Northampton, Mass.: Smith College Museum of Art, 1979.

Nicoll, Allardyce. *The Development of the Theatre.* 4th ed., rev. London: George G. Harrap & Company, 1959.

Ogden, Dunbar H. *The Italian Baroque Stage.* Berkeley: University of California Press, 1978.

Portraits of the American Stage: 1771-1971, exh. cat. Washington, D.C.: Smithsonian Institution Press for The National Portrait Gallery, 1971.

Reade, Brian. *Art Nouveau and Alphonse Mucha.* London: Her Majesty's Stationery Office, 1967.

Reade, Brian. *Ballet Designs and Illustrations 1581-1940: A Catalogue Raisonné.* London: Her Majesty's Stationery Office for Victoria and Albert Museum, 1967.

Reff, Theodore. "Edgar Degas and the Dance," in *Arts Magazine* 53 (November 1978), 145-49.

Rischbieter, Henning, ed., *Art and the Stage in the 20th Century.* Greenwich, Conn.: New York Graphic Society, 1968.

Rood, Arnold. *Edward Gordon Craig: Artist of the Theatre 1872-1966,* exh. cat. New York: New York Public Library, 1967. Memorial exhibition at the Amsterdam Gallery, Lincoln Center; introduction by Donald Oenslager.

Rubenstein, Daryl R. *The Avant-Garde in Theatre and Art: French Playbills of the 1890s,* exh. cat. Washington, D.C.: Smithsonian Institution Traveling Exhibition Service, 1972.

Russell, Douglas A. *Theatrical Style: A Visual Approach to the Theatre.* Palo Alto, Calif.: Mayfield Publishing Company, 1976.

Russian Theater and Costume Designs, exh. cat. San Francisco: The Fine Arts Museums of San Francisco, 1979. Introduction by John E. Bowlt.

Schlemmer, Oskar: Moholy-Nagy, Laszlo; and Molnar, Farkas. *The Theater of the Bauhaus.* Middletown, Conn.: Wesleyan University Press, 1961. Edited and with introduction by Walter Gropius.

Scholz, Janus, ed. *Baroque and Romantic Stage Design.* New York: H. Bittner and Co., 1950.

Seligman, Germain. *The Drawings of Georges Seurat.* New York: Curt Valentin, 1947.

Seurat: Paintings and Drawings, exh. cat. Chicago: The Art Institute of Chicago, 1958. Edited and with essay by Daniel Catton Rich; essay by Robert L. Herbert.

Simonson, Lee. *Theatre Art,* exh. cat. New York: W. W. Norton and Company for The Museum of Modern Art, 1934.

Spritz, Kenneth. *Theatrical Evolution: 1776-1976,* exh. cat. Yonkers, N.Y.: The Hudson River Museum at Yonkers, 1976.

Stuckey, Charles F. *Toulouse-Lautrec: Paintings,* exh. cat. Chicago: The Art Institute of Chicago, 1980.

Sweeny, Barbara. *Toulouse-Lautrec,* exh. cat. Philadelphia: Philidelphia Museum of Art, 1955.

Theatrical Drawings and Watercolors by George Grosz, exh. cat. Boston: Busch-Reisinger Museum, 1973.

Thompson, Richard. *Toulouse-Lautrec.* London: Oresko Books, 1977.

Tisdall, Caroline and Bozzolla, Angelo. *Futurism.* New York and Toronto: Oxford University Press, 1978.

Toulouse-Lautrec, 1864-1901, exh. cat. Montreal: The Montreal Museum of Fine Arts, 1968. Preface by Jean Adhémar: introduction by Luc d'Iberville-Moreau.

Whistler: Themes and Variations, exh. cat. Stanford, Calif.: Stanford University Museum of Art, 1978.